WITHDRAWN

The Andrew R. Cecil Lectures on

Moral Values in a Free Society

established by

The University of Texas at Dallas

Volume XI

Previous Volumes of the Andrew R. Cecil Lectures on Moral Values in a Free Society

OUR ECONOMIC SYSTEM:
ITS STRENGTHS AND WEAKNESSES

Our Economic System: Its Strengths and Weaknesses

EDWIN L. ARTZT
JON LOVELACE
ELMER W. JOHNSON
J. EDWARD FOWLER
BENJAMIN AARON
ANDREW R. CECIL

With an Introduction by
ANDREW R. CECIL

Edited by
W. LAWSON TAITTE

The University of Texas at Dallas
1990

HB
72
.687
1990
14 9937
Dec.1990

Library of Congress Catalog Card Number 90-070936
International Standard Book Number 0-292-76033-7

Distributed by The University of Texas Press,
Box 7819, Austin, Texas 78712

FOREWORD

The University of Texas at Dallas established the Andrew R. Cecil Lectures on Moral Values in a Free Society in 1979 in order to provide a forum for the discussion of the important issues that confront our society. Each year since then the University has invited scholars, business leaders, and public officials to its campus to share their ideas with the academic community and the general public. The Cecil Lectures have become a valued tradition not only for U. T. Dallas but for the wider community. The prominent authorities in many fields who have participated in this program have contributed positively to our understanding of the system of moral values on which our country was founded. In offering the Lectures on Moral Values in a Free Society, the University is discharging an important responsibility.

The University named this program for Dr. Andrew R. Cecil, its Distinguished Scholar in Residence. During his tenure as President of The Southwestern Legal Foundation, Dr. Cecil's innovative leadership brought that institution into the forefront of continuing legal education in the United States. When he retired from the Foundation as its Chancellor Emeritus, Dr. Cecil was asked by The University of Texas at Dallas to serve as its Distinguished Scholar in Residence, and the Cecil Lectures were instituted. It is appropriate that they honor a man who has been concerned throughout his career with the moral foundations of our society and has stressed his belief in the dignity and worth of every individual.

The eleventh annual series of the Cecil Lectures

was held on the campus of the University on November 13 through 16, 1989. The theme of the 1989 Lectures was "Our Economic System: Its Strengths and Weaknesses." On behalf of U. T. Dallas, I would like to express our gratitude to Mr. Edwin L. Artzt, to Mr. Jon Lovelace, to Mr. Elmer W. Johnson, to Mr. J. Edward Fowler, to Professor Benjamin Aaron, and to Dr. Cecil for their willingness to share their ideas and for the outstanding lectures that are preserved in these proceedings.

U. T. Dallas also wishes to express its appreciation to all those who have helped make this program an important part of the life of the University, especially the contributors to the program. By their support these donors enable us to continue this important project and to publish the proceedings of the series, thus assuring a wide and permanent audience for the ideas they contain.

I know that everyone who reads *Our Economic System: Its Strengths and Weaknesses*, the Andrew R. Cecil Lectures on Moral Values in a Free Society Volume XI, will be stimulated by the ideas presented in the six lectures it contains.

ROBERT H. RUTFORD, President
The University of Texas at Dallas
May 1990

CONTENTS

INTRODUCTION
by
Andrew R. Cecil

Alexis de Tocqueville in his conclusion to the first part of the *Democratie* (published in Paris in 1835) made an amazing prophecy: "Two great peoples," he wrote—the Russians and the Americans—would "reach the first rank of nations," and although their "ways are diverse, yet each of them was called by the secret design of Providence to control, some day, the destinies of half the world." No less amazing is the prophecy Tocqueville gave about the courses that the two nations would follow to power:

> "The American battles the obstacles of nature; the Russians, those of man. . . . To attain its ends, the American relies upon personal interest and allows free scope to the unguided energy and common sense of individuals. The Russian somehow concentrates the power of society in one man. The method of the former is freedom; of the latter servitude."

We do live in one of the freest lands upon the earth, and history provides evidence that the open road to prosperity is a system that rewards the initiative of the free entrepreneur. Some other nations, including those under communist regimes, are only now starting to experiment with the free enterprise system that has been the basis for our economic success.

It cannot, however, be stressed enough that eco-

11

nomic structures do not exist in a moral vacuum. For economic growth and progress to flourish over the long run, it is essential that business leadership combine self-interest with attention to the public interest. Signs of self-destruction inevitably appear when selfish desires for the attainment of power over others or for special privileges take priority over a businessman's responsibility for the welfare of his fellowman and of the society at large. History teaches us that what is morally wrong cannot be economically right in the long run.

History also teaches us that economic strength, like military power, tends to have a limited cycle of life. When each of these has risen to its highest levels, it may fall precipitously if the society that has built it up abandons the sources to which such strength should be attributed. Our own national situation provokes the troubling question of whether the bastion of our economic strength has become vulnerable to the same sort of forces that led to the downward cycles experienced by great powers in the past. Are we heading, economically, in the direction of decline that befell the military strength of Napoleon's France or of the nineteenth-century British empire?

The alternating periods of prosperity and depressions resulting from irregularly recurring economic fluctuations are known as business cycles. Many theories have been offered to explain the causes of these cycles, including even theories pointing at factors outside economic life, such as sunspots (which also come and go in cycles). None of these theories, however, has proved to be an all-inclusive explanation. Evidence increasingly suggests that economic decline—the cyclic repetition of the miseries of recession and depression—is not an incurable disease that cannot be prevented, nor is it a violent shock like an earthquake. Recession and depression can be avoided by preventive measures. The course of economic life is not decreed by nature, and modern society has the ability to shape its own economic destiny.

We are witnessing a great change in our understanding of what it means to have a "free economy." While we continue to advocate the blessings of a free market, we have delegated to the Group of Seven (United States, Great Britain, Canada, France, Germany, Italy, and Japan) the coordination of the monetary exchange market. The "G-7" governments have become engaged not only in the coordination of their monetary policies but also in finding solutions to issues concerning the internal economic structure of their respective countries.

When on October 13, 1989, the Dow Jones Industrial Average plunged 190.58 points, the Federal Reserve Board and the U. S. Treasury advised the proper officials here and abroad that our central bank was prepared to pour massive amounts of money into the banking system to prevent a financial crisis. The central bank assumed the same role in October 1987 by providing the market with the money necessary to keep the financial system afloat. Such money becomes available when the central bank buys government securities from financial institutions. The delegation to government officials of the monitoring of events as they unfold in financial markets around the world and a readiness of the central bank to inject large amounts of funds into the stock market are patterns hardly consistent with doctrinaire and simplistic concepts of a "free economy" and a free market governed solely by the law of supply and demand.

In the United States, the 1980s were marked by sustained economic growth, the creation of millions of new jobs, low inflation, low interest rates, and low unemployment. But that decade was also a period when the United States, once the world's largest creditor, became the world's largest debtor by spending more than it produced and when Japan became the globe's richest creditor. The state of the U. S. economy has other problems as well. Its flaws include constant budget deficits, trade deficits, volatile exchange rates, failing banks and savings and loan institutions, stock scandals caused by the corruption of traders and high-placed industry officials, consumer credit debt dangerously outgrowing the rate of savings, and the proliferation of leveraged buyouts (LBOs) that have caused an explosion of corporate debt and become a hot political issue.

The United States still maintains its position as the largest economic entity in the world, but the above-mentioned signs of weakness warrant real concern. This concern is augmented by the plans of the European Community to achieve a completely integrated internal market by the end of 1992. The objective of full liberalization of the movement of goods, services, capital, and people is to make Europe more competitive in the world trade market that is daily becoming harsher through the growing competition between the major economic regions. This concern

is also augmented by the fact that the Japanese private savings ratio is at least triple the level of savings
in the United States. The savings of the private sector in Japan finance not only the government deficit
but also investments in the Japanese economy, as well
as strong foreign investment.

In light of far-reaching economic growth and massive expansion of economic development in many
areas of the world (not only in Japan and Europe),
we must ask ourselves whether we in the United
States can close the three gaps that together imperil
our economic strength: the import-export gap, the
output-spending gap, and the savings-investment gap.
Our solutions to these problems will in large part determine the answer to the question, What lies ahead
of us?

In his address in the 1989 Lectures on Moral
Values in a Free Society entitled "The Future of Free
Enterprise in the Next Century," Mr. Edwin L. Artzt
looks over the road lying ahead of us from the perspective of a business leader. He takes note of important recent developments and sees both the
promise and the danger that they entail. In his view,
the most important truth that business leaders must
keep in mind in planning for the future is the increasing global interdependence of all nations. This
interdependence has a great impact on such issues
as the environment and the needs of less-developed
nations, as well as on the marketing and production
strategies of individual corporations.

Mr. Artzt sees a number of opportunities for
American businesses in this globalization of the economy. Worldwide markets will enable strong busi-

nesses to continue to grow, and the American traditions of initiative and innovation will provide a spark
for such growth. Of course, companies will have success in the new worldwide economy only if they learn
to make their staffs and ways of thinking truly international and if the ideal of free international trade
continues to become a more practical reality on a
day-to-day basis.

Mr. Artzt's lecture offers a glimpse of the new
challenges that will mark the start of the next decade
and of the twenty-first century. To make the vision
of the life of tomorrow still clearer, we also have to
ask the question of what moral values will have to
undergird the U. S. economy in order for it to remain a preeminent force while the economies of
other nations continue to expand. Will moral values
be included in the business world's agenda at the
turn of the next century?

Mr. Jon Lovelace in his lecture "Moral and Ethical Values Within the U. S. Economic System in a
Global Context" notes that many businessmen are
now paying increasing attention to the question of
ethical and moral values. Many areas of a nation's
strength also imply a corresponding weakness or vulnerability, and Mr. Lovelace observes that that is true
for the United States. Our legal system, with its dedication to a consistent code of laws and procedures
ensuring impartial justice, can lead to a legalistic
rather than truly moral outlook on an individual's
or a company's actions. The emphasis may then shift
to the question of whether an action is legal rather
than whether it is right.

Emphasizing, like Mr. Artzt, the globalization of

the world's economy, Mr. Lovelace examines the trade conflicts between the United States and Japan with respect to the underlying values systems of the two nations. Differing cultural presuppositions may result in harmful failures in communication. He also discusses the impact of the new global, twenty-four-hour securities trading markets on the international economic system and concludes that unrecognized opportunities for abuse exist. Two other important matters are also of concern to Mr. Lovelace: the impact of leveraged buyouts and increasingly short-term planning on our global competitiveness, and the need for increased awareness of environmental issues.

In spite of concern about these two matters and about its rising debt, the United States can retain its preeminent global leadership in the great power race if Americans exhibit the will to lead in redirecting the downward cycle that doomsayers predict will be both an era of decline for America and an era of the replacement of our country by new leaders in the world's economy. In the coming era of competition that, one hopes, is replacing the era of confrontation between the superpowers, the United States has the resources to win the global economic contest.

Nothing has ever been built on pessimism, and there are reasons for being cautiously optimistic about the future, since the United States has never ceased to be the land of unlimited opportunities. We are once again able, for instance, to match the military strength of the Soviet Union, while the Moscow leaders admit their economic failures, including constantly slowing industrial and agricultural growth.

Also, America's gross national product is more than twice the size of Japan's. Furthermore, the Japanese system of values based on loyalty, industriousness, conformity, and obedience may have ingredients that will influence other nations, but because of the great disparities between the cultures and economies of Asian nations, there will always be a reluctance, even in Asia, to accept Japanese leadership. The wartime brutalities Japan inflicted on neighboring countries, still vivid in the memories of many Asians, do not provide a favorable climate for a viable economic bloc. Even the foreign aid program offered by Japan (which in 1989 made it the world's largest donor and lender) is accepted by African and Asian nations with the suspicion that the disbursement of funds is influenced by Japan's trading interests rather than directed by concern about the essential needs of the recipient nations.

A unified Europe, with its highly educated human resources that are more numerous than America's, may become a powerful competitor and share a large part of the global output, but it will take generations before it achieves the political unity that has added so much to America's strength. Europe may be able to claim that the United States has not developed as many economic and political theorists as Europe, but the important fact is that our pragmatism has been crowned with impressive achievements.

In his lecture "Ethics and Corporate Governance in the Age of Pension Fund Capitalism," Mr. Elmer W. Johnson inquires into the roots of these achievements and finds that one of the important sources of the success of American capitalism is "patient capital"—the willingness of some investors to take a long-range view of the potential of the company they have invested in. Mr. Johnson argues that several developments in recent decades have imperiled this record of success: the growth of bureaucracy in major corporations, a top-down management style, and a growing passivity in Boards of Directors. These forces, along with an extremely rapid turnover of stock ownership (largely the result of huge institutional investors, such as pension funds), have resulted in a myopic capitalism—one that considers only short-range results.

Mr. Johnson offers several possible remedies to these problems. He believes that Boards of Directors should be much smaller and that outside directors could become something like ombudsmen within the structures of their companies, representing newly diverse points of view. In Mr. Johnson's opinion, directors should be required to own a significant number of shares in their companies, companies should foster a sense of ownership in their management, and boards should assume responsibility for the overall policies of investment of their pension funds. Only when those who nominally oversee our great corporations take their responsibilities seriously will we witness improvement in the conditions in our economic system that are now cause for alarm.

To improve these conditions and to maintain world leadership, we should eliminate the separation that has appeared in modern times between ethical ideals and economic policy and behavior. Although economic efficiency is indispensable to the success of a businessman, such success cannot endure when it is divorced from moral considerations and when the businessman's activities violate the rights of his fellowmen. No economic action can be sound and fruitful without an accepted system of values. In order to succeed economically, a businessman must channel his efforts, talents, energies, and intelligence into avenues that will lead his business to prosper. His efforts, however, must be combined with a responsibility for promoting the well-being of the society in which he lives.

Giant takeovers, mergers, and acquisitions; mammoth leveraged buyouts financed through "junk bonds" paying very high interest rates reflecting their high risks; and guilty pleas to criminal fraud by LBO fund managers remind us of the warning by John Maynard Keynes in *The General Theory of Employment, Interest, and Money*:

> "When the capital development of a country becomes a product of the activities of a casino, the job is likely to be ill-done. The measure of success attained by Wall Street . . . cannot be claimed as one of the outstanding triumphs of laissez-faire capitalism."

Corporate executives have important responsibilities to protect the corporation from becoming involved in wheeling-and-dealing speculative games and to enhance business activities that are of benefit to the shareholders and the national economy.

Mr. J. Edward Fowler in his lecture "Corporate Governance Issues in the Takeover Era" examines the history of the modern corporation and the theoretical assumptions that lie behind the most common attitudes toward the governance of these corporations. His examination includes a review of an essential question that has been asked in our own century, namely, Who actually owns a publicly held corporation? In earlier decades, it was assumed that the stockholders, since they owned the shares in the company, were in fact the only ones who properly held a legal and moral interest in the affairs of the company. More recently, it has been argued that others—including the managers and employees of the corporation and, to a lesser extent, the general public—have a legitimate claim to have a voice in the way a corporation does its business.

The leveraged buyout often reaps great profit for investors but can devastate the others who have an interest in the corporation. Because of recent decisions in the courts of Delaware (where many corporations are chartered) and other recent developments, Mr. Fowler holds out hope that the legitimate interests of stockholders, as well as those of other "stakeholders" in a corporation and of society at large, will be balanced in an effort to achieve well-considered and socially responsible business strategies.

Business strategy includes labor relations. In discussing the responsibilities of management, we should always keep in mind that labor relations have a direct impact on economic growth, inflation, international trade, and the stability of the economy. One of the responsibilities of labor and management is to protect the uniqueness of the special endowment of the individuality of each worker. Although

a person's physical presence can be bought, en-
thusiasm, initiative, and loyalty are not for sale. These
intangible qualities must be earned. In order to unleash the creative energy with which we are endowed,
we have to strive for the common welfare by providing greater opportunity and security to each individual engaged in economic activity. This kind of
welfare calls for the right of workers, along with all
other citizens, to share in the advancing prosperity
of the nation.

In his lecture "Labor and the Economy: Toward
a 'Kinder and Gentler' Society," Professor Benjamin
Aaron argues that in the last decade insufficient attention has been paid to the interests of workers, especially those workers who are most disadvantaged.
He notes the growing incidence of high-school
dropouts and teenage pregnancy and sees a need for
increased attention to job training. He believes that
the minimum wage is currently too low and that recent attempts to raise the wage have been halfheart-
ed and insufficient.

Other areas of concern to Professor Aaron are a
need for increased employment security for workers
and for more liberal policies of family and medical
leave. Like so many others of the 1989 lecturers, he
is also concerned about the effects of LBOs on our
economic system. Unlike some of our other lecturers,
however, Professor Aaron believes that the primary
remedy for the problems he discusses is legislative.
Only if the country is willing to invest in seeking solutions to these problems is an amelioration in them
likely.

In my lecture on "Equality," I have tried to explain

the distinctive American concept of equality in freedom, which differs dramatically from the European passion for egalitarianism—a passion that has often given birth to bloody revolution. When such a revolution succeeds, the new rules it institutes take the place of those of the previous oppressors, and the new regime often proves to be crueler and more barbaric than the government that went before.

The American concept of equality calls for an equality of conditions that gives each citizen equal opportunity to make his own place in society, since all people are created with equal rights that are not conferred by the state and cannot be denied by it. The egalitarian concept of equality calls for a common level of wealth and income, for equally distributed rewards, and for an absolute equality of results. These principles lead to an equality of slaves who live under a government offering brutal repression.

Equality in freedom offers each person the opportunity to rise as high as merit will carry him. A free society, however, to some extent is destined to be an unequal one because all men are not created equal in talent. A person's status depends upon such qualities as creativity, industriousness, extra efforts, and special abilities.

In the 1989 Lectures on Moral Values in a Free Society, the theme is repeatedly stressed that economic activities cannot be divorced from moral considerations, even in an extreme and severe analysis. When transferred to totalitarian countries, machines and tools such as those used by the free world produce only a fraction of the goods they supply a free society. The possibilities of machines are limited. It is high moral standards and inspiring leadership that provide the incentives that permit society to benefit from the unlimited possibilities of the individual.

The concept "economics is one thing, moral values are another" is false. Morality and economics cannot be locked up in separate compartments with no vital connection with one another. Economic activities cannot be judged only by abstract economic criteria, since moral traditions do not exist in a vacuum or in a world apart but rather have their impact on all human conduct, including the conduct of business. Habits of living acquired by individuals, professions, groups of people, or even nations are the results of the conditions in which people live. These conditions include the spiritual and moral environment.

THE FUTURE OF
FREE ENTERPRISE
IN THE NEXT CENTURY

by

Edwin L. Artzt

Edwin L. Artzt

Edwin L. Artzt is Chairman of the Board and Chief Executive of the Procter & Gamble Company. Mr. Artzt joined Procter & Gamble in 1953, becoming Vice President in the Paper Products Division in 1969 and joining the Board of Directors in 1972 and again in 1980. His service with the company has included extensive experience in Europe, where he served as Group Vice President for European Operations.

Mr. Artzt was educated at the University of Oregon. He serves as a director for GTE Corporation and Teradyne, Inc.

Among many other civic activities, Mr. Artzt serves on the Board of Governors of the Joseph H. Lauder Institute of Management & International Studies at The Wharton School of the University of Pennsylvania; on the Board of Directors of the National Foreign Trade Council, Inc.; on the Board of Trustees and as a Member of the Executive Committee of the U. S. Council for International Business; and as a Member of the U. S. Joint Working Group on the U. S.-Japan Agenda of the Center for Strategic & International Studies in Washington, D. C. He is a member of the Council on Foreign Relations, the National Council for United States-China Trade, the Canadian-American Committee, and the Advisory Group on Capital Development for Mexico of the Council of the Americas. Mr. Artzt speaks frequently at business schools throughout the country.

THE FUTURE OF
FREE ENTERPRISE
IN THE NEXT CENTURY
by
Edwin L. Artzt

Normally, when I speak at a university, my job is
to deliver a sales pitch—to persuade the audience
that there's no better place on earth to work than
Procter & Gamble. My job in this lecture is somewhat
different—namely, to persuade you that free enterprise is the best hope for worldwide stability and
prosperity in the twenty-first century. Assuming that
I do not have to work too hard to convince you on
that point, I would like to describe some of the forces
that will affect free enterprise. Then I would like to
outline at least one scenario which I believe will help
ensure the future of the free enterprise system.

As you will soon discover, I am neither a philosopher nor a scholar like Dr. Cecil. I am a businessman. Therefore, I come at this subject with a
businessman's agenda. I start with the conviction that
free enterprise is the only system of economic development that has, over several centuries, advanced
civilization, advanced human achievement, and advanced world peace.

Communism, with its centrally planned econom-
ic system, is in disarray. In fact, there is a real crisis
in the communist system today, and the crisis is
erupting all around us—in China, in the Soviet
Union, in East Germany—and throughout the War-
saw Pact bloc of nations.

In the past, we have defined free enterprise in national terms. Some countries had free enterprise systems; some did not. And the words "free enterprise" were almost synonymous with "American."

Today we are at the beginning of a new era—the era of the global economy. If free enterprise is to survive, we must have greater cooperation among governments. We must be able to move goods and capital freely from nation to nation, from supplier to customer, from producer to consumer, wherever in the world they may be.

This really is not a new thought. Even after 213 years, the philosophy of Adam Smith in *The Wealth of Nations* is still applicable. He wrote, "Both parties to an exchange can benefit and . . . so long as cooperation is strictly voluntary, no exchange will take place unless both parties do benefit."

Adam Smith did not have the advantage of the analytical tools at our disposal: the information systems; global telecommunications, broadly shared; and easily accessible worldwide knowledge. Yet he knew something then that the governments of the world have trouble understanding today. He said, "No external force, no coercion, no violation of freedom is necessary to produce cooperation among individuals all of whom can benefit."

We want to believe that this theory is true. But it is often not applied. Nations continue to impose regulations that discriminate against foreign investors. Nations continue to levy tariffs to block imports. Nations continue to enact legislation that tries to ensure that they benefit from world trade more than other countries do. These kinds of controls are the enemy of cooperation. They represent the greatest threat to the future of free enterprise.

What, then, is the probable future of the free enterprise system? What will it look like in, say, 2020? Let's think about that. Here is one scenario: The year is 2020, about 30 years from now. In Washington, the Republicans are in the White House and the Democrats control the Congress. Nothing new here. All twenty-five of the world's largest banks are Japanese. That could happen. Most metropolitan real estate is owned by non-U. S. citizens, principally Japanese. Many leading U. S. enterprises are owned by foreign interests, particularly British, German, and Japanese. That could happen, too, and probably will.

But that concerns me, because the more U. S. companies become branches of foreign companies, the more that inevitably blocks the globalization of American enterprise. A key premise in my remarks is that the successful globalization of American enterprise is critical to ensuring the future of the free enterprise system in the twenty-first century and beyond.

Let's continue our crystal ball visit to the year 2020. In the United States, sushi has replaced the hamburger as the favorite American fast food. In Japan, the Big Mac has replaced sushi as that country's favorite fast food. Free trade's finest hour! The Dallas Cowboys have won the fifty-fourth Super Bowl, and the Cincinnati Reds, my home team, are in fifth place in the National League West.

Whether you share my vision or not, I think you would agree that this is a scenario in which life goes on without much change—except perhaps for the Dallas Cowboys.

But what changes might occur that could threaten the future of our free enterprise system? If I were a pessimist—and I am not—I might conjure up a chilling vision of the year 2020.

In that scenario, the U. S. trade balance would be worse than ever. The U. S. budget deficit would have defied Gramm-Rudman and would exceed $300 billion per year, $5 trillion on a cumulative basis. The United States would have become one of the highest-risk debtor nations, with annual interest rates of 25–35 percent. Europe, in the 30 years since 1990, would have become a fortress, virtually closing its borders to outside world trade—while Asia, somewhat in defense, would have formed a regional, multilateral trading bloc.

The General Agreement on Tariffs and Trade, known as GATT, would have broken down, and countries would have created new barriers to trade and investment. Latin America and other less-developed countries, isolated from the failure of GATT, would all have repudiated their foreign debt and made a sharp turn to the left politically.

Eastern Europe, finding little access to the world's richer markets, would have failed to find political stability, and repression would have overcome reform. The dreams of economic progress and transition to market-driven economies would have faded with the events of Tiananmen Square in China and the subsequent failure of Gorbachev to rescue his country's bankrupt economy.

I don't expect any of this to happen, but it could. And I don't think any of us want our grandchildren and great-grandchildren to inherit a world that looks like that.

Fortunately, recorded history proves that it is the drive of the human spirit that motivates economic success. Even under the most repressive conditions, people will work to improve their lives. Through that drive, they better themselves, and they better society.

It is going on everywhere. Right now. In just a few short months, events of incredible magnitude have rocked the world and reminded us of the power of the human spirit. The courage of the citizens of Beijing and the students in Tiananmen Square, the persistence of the Solidarity party in Poland, the millions of oppressed pouring out of East Germany—all these phenomena prove that people want better lives and that they will not long tolerate systems that fail to meet their basic expectations, no matter how powerful a government's hold may be.

The collapse of the Berlin Wall is more than just a blow for freedom. It is a blow against industrial inefficiency, low productivity, waste, poor quality, high costs, shortages, and a failure to deal with social and environmental problems.

The free enterprise system faces the same issues, the same problems. Will it face the same fate? Not if we keep it free—truly free—and fully adaptable to the growing interdependence of nations for their social and economic welfare.

What does that mean? For one thing, it means that we must deal globally with issues of the environment. Private enterprise must shoulder its share of the burden and not wait for governments to regulate the protection of our land, air, water, and other natural resources.

It also means that we must deal globally with the issues of hunger and economic oppression, and private enterprise has a burden to share there as well. I am one of those who believe that the greatest threat to the future of our free enterprise system is not the emergence of communist or socialist centrally managed economic systems in the world. Rather, it is the lack of development and investment in the highly populous, seriously underdeveloped, debt-ridden, struggling nations of the world.

One of the greatest challenges to be faced in the next century is the prospect of a major food shortage. The world population will be more than 5 billion in 1990, and it is projected to increase to 6.25 billion by the year 2000. Most of this growth will come in the less-developed countries. (Lester R. Brown, "Feeding Six Billion," *Grain*, Oct. 1989, p. 34 ff.)

Just think of it: 88 million new people every year between now and the year 2000, and they all have to eat. Yet the world faces a growing scarcity of usable cropland, an increased soil erosion problem, and diminishing supplies of water for agricultural irrigation. Clearly, the resources of the free enterprise system—technology, capital, and entrepreneurial initiative—are required to meet this enormous consumer need.

The point I am making is that we cannot think of the future of our free enterprise system only in political and socioeconomic terms. Issues of the environment and the needs of the less-developed countries of the world must be dealt with globally, and with the full participation of private enterprise, if our system is to remain healthy.

Having said all that, there is one issue that in my mind stands above the rest. It is a healthy United States. In fact, nothing is more important to ensure the future of free enterprise worldwide than to strengthen the global competitiveness of American business. This is something we can all do something about.

This conclusion is supported by a report from the Steering Group headed by Senator Bill Bradley and former Senator and Cabinet official Bill Brock. The group, organized in May 1989 by the Center for Strategic and International Studies, said:

> "There is no prospect for sustained growth and an improved standard of living in the United States without our being fully engaged and competitive in world markets. Our national economic strategy needs to be geared to maintaining our competitive edge in world trade. American business leaders need to make exports and foreign investment central to their corporate strategies. Our trade policy needs to ensure open and stable access to markets abroad." (Ernest R. Preeg, "The American Challenge in World Trade," *Center for Strategic and International Studies, Significant Issues Series,* Vol. XI, No. 7, p. xi.)

That is exactly what we are trying to do at Procter & Gamble. Naturally, my own company is the enterprise about which I know the most, and I shall try

to illustrate some of the kinds of things that I believe
are necessary for international competitiveness by
discussing its efforts in this regard. My company's
plans are based on the assumption that the markets
of the world are open to our enterprise. In fact, we
are banking on it.

For those of you who may be unfamiliar with Procter & Gamble, I would like to provide a little background. Our sales are about $21 billion world-
wide—60 percent in the United States and 40 percent internationally. We sell a total of 165 brands in
140 countries, mostly through wholly owned subsidi-
aries with headquarters on the ground in the 45 largest countries. More than two-thirds of our business
internationally is done in what we call "world
brands," products like Crest toothpaste, Head &
Shoulders shampoo, Pampers disposable diapers,
Vicks cold remedy, and many others.

This focus on selling world brands in most of the
world's markets has caused us to think globally about
our business. It has required us to become a globally competitive company. What do we see, then, as we
look to the twenty-first century? What will our business environment be like? What will our company
look like? We should, of course, be a great deal larger. If we keep expanding our company at the same
compound growth rates as in the decade of the 1980s,
Procter & Gamble will have more than $50 billion
in sales and $3 billion in earnings by the twenty-first
century.

The United States will remain P&G's most important market, and our largest contributor to profit,
and we consider that a great asset. First of all, our

U. S. brands and businesses have always been the primary wellspring of new ideas and technology for reapplication worldwide, and we expect that to continue. In fact, one of our company's greatest competitive advantages is having the United States as our home market. It gives us direct access to more volume, more profit, and more talent than any of our global competitors.

I also believe that the better we do here, the better we can expect to do internationally and thus worldwide. I cannot think of anything I would rather be than a successful American company facing the challenges of a global free enterprise system in the next century. At the same time, we expect the international part of our business to grow larger and account for more than half of our worldwide total by the end of the 1990s.

The business world around us will change, too. We can expect a continuing pattern of mergers and acquisitions, joint ventures, and other strategic alliances. Competition will be more concentrated in fewer, larger, more sophisticated companies.

We will be facing more European and Japanese competition in the United States and more Japanese competition in Europe. I expect, too, that ownership of U. S. companies, like globally oriented European and Japanese multinationals, will continue to rise. But the same is true of our customers and our suppliers—more concentration in fewer hands and more ownership here in the United States by globally sophisticated multinationals. Today, nearly 20 percent of the U. S. grocery trade is already owned by European companies that operate in dozens of countries. That number could easily double in the 1990s as the Japanese expand into U. S. retailing.

Customer alignment, a major principle in our company, will be well established worldwide. By the year 2000, this alignment will undoubtedly be dealing with customers on a worldwide basis—customers who will be made up of consortiums of companies capable of exporting and importing goods to their members in all parts of the world.

Product supply systems will change, too, as trade barriers come down all over the world. The one-market concept of Europe, beginning in 1993, should expand to include Eastern Europe and the Soviet Union by the end of the decade.

What an opportunity these markets represent to the free enterprise system. The Soviet Union, for example, faces the enormously difficult task of trying to convert from a centrally planned to a market-driven economic system—with the help of private enterprise from the West and the Far East. In the Eastern bloc, we are dealing with economic systems where everything has been subsidized. Nobody knows what anything costs, and the people in charge have little, if any, experience in managing efficient, profitable operation. Our company wants to be part of the transformation that has to take place in the economies of Eastern Europe. We may not see a Western-style free enterprise system in these countries in our lifetime, but we will see them improve the quality of their products and their supply systems, which will enable them to invest in and trade with the rest of the world.

The Far East is increasingly becoming a market, and global companies, such as ours, are setting up product supply structures to optimize the flow of goods from country to country.

Product supply will change in North America, too. The U. S./Canada Trade Agreement, which phases in over the next 5 to 10 years, will be matched, in my view, by some kind of bilateral trade agreement with Mexico. Our company is thus taking steps now to coordinate product supply planning on a North American basis. We expect that during the 1990s we will see a sharp increase in North/South cross-border flows of products.

The trend toward globalization of markets and integration of economies will also affect the way businesses structure their organizations and communicate internally. A new culture of professional managers and technicians will transcend national borders and languages. They will communicate, primarily in English, in global rather than national terms. This is already happening to a great extent. Within Procter & Gamble, we see these managers and other professionals becoming more diverse. Our management ranks will have greater numbers of women, minorities, and employees from our international companies.

How can we make certain that American companies are among the world leaders in the 1990s and on into the next century? I discussed this topic with Procter & Gamble employees at our most recent annual year-end meetings. We agreed that one of our key objectives for the next decade is to continue progress in the globalization of our company. What does that mean? It means changing from a United States-based business that sells some of its products

in international markets into a truly world company, a company that thinks of everything it does in
terms of the entire world.

How will globalization affect the way we run our
business? We will increasingly plan the growth of our
business and our technology investments on a worldwide basis. Globalization, however, does not mean
that we plan to run our business globally. That would
not work. We will manage our business and our
brands regionally and locally. As far out in the future as I can see, we are still going to be selling our
brands one at a time to each individual customer in
his or her local store. How well we do will depend
on how much better we are than our competitors at
satisfying consumers' needs and their demand for
quality, no matter where they live.

Global planning, however, will become a major
part of Procter & Gamble's business strategies. It will
help us leverage our strong presence throughout the
world to earn maximum return on our investment
in product research. It will help us gain maximum
benefit from what we learn, and it will greatly help
us plan the strategic deployment of our talent and
resources for maximum competitive advantage.

Globalization also means bringing a worldwide
perspective to our U. S. business. The United States
is not only our most important market, it is the number one target market of every global company. Our
competitors from abroad bring their technology, experience, and worldwide perspectives here and
deploy them against us—just as we have done to them
overseas. In fact, we owe much of the success of our
international business today to the brands, the ideas,

and the product initiatives that were developed here in the United States and adapted overseas.

We need to make sure that this same advantage flows in both directions and that all our U. S. functions are thoroughly up-to-date, completely informed, and well plugged in to what is going on in our company in their areas of the business worldwide. We are talking about more than information sharing. We are talking about working closely together to plan business strategies on a worldwide basis.

Globalization, of course, also means that we will continue to place high priority on the expansion of our international business. We want to make sure that we have the strongest possible infrastructure to market our world brands and to exploit our world-class technology to enter new categories in all the world's key markets. Globalization also means increasing the focus of research and development on technology that can be readily reapplied and tailored to fit our business needs everywhere. Furthermore, it means globalizing our sources of innovation. Procter & Gamble, for instance, will soon be under way with the construction of a new technical center in Japan, and this will see us have major capacity for product and packaging innovation in the Far East, as well as the United States, the United Kingdom, and continental Europe.

Of course, we can spout globalization until we are blue in the face, and the cause of free enterprise will be poorly served unless the world is open to our business. Trade barriers inhibit free enterprise. They especially penalize American business, because our

markets are open to all foreign competitors. Therefore, what *we* do is not enough. What *we* do as global
companies to strengthen American competitiveness
worldwide is not enough to ensure the future stability of our system. There must be significant cooperation from the governments of the trading nations
of the world. The means to that are at hand in the
vital GATT Uruguay Round world trade negotiations
now under way in Geneva.

We strongly support the efforts of the U. S. government and the Uruguay Round to bring about multilateral leveling of the world's playing fields. The
GATT is not a perfect process. It has severe critics
among the more protectionist nations, but clearly the
GATT and the current Uruguay Round negotiations
are the best and only hope for making the much-
needed improvements in the way the world's trading system operates.

The United States Trade Representative, Ambassador Carla Hills, made that very point when she addressed the Organization for Economic Cooperation
and Development Ministerial Meeting last May. She
said, "The GATT needs reform. It must speak to the
21st Century. A successful Uruguay Round is vital to
a healthy, growing trading system in the decades
ahead." (Carla A. Hills, Statement by United States
Trade Representative, May 31, 1989, p. 2.) In a later
statement in London, Ambassador Hills set forth the
policy of the current administration when she said,
"Our policy is to open markets, not to close them;
to create an ever-expanding global trading system
based upon clear and enforceable rules." (Hills, "The
Uruguay Round and U. S. Trade Policy: A Founda-

tion for the Future," Statement by United States
Representative, Sept. 14, 1989, p. 2 ff.)
What kinds of clear and enforceable rules are we
seeking?

The U. S. goal is to ensure market access for industrial products, for equity capital, and for foreign investment.

In agriculture, the goal is to eliminate all trade-
distorting measures and subsidies on a schedule
that gives farmers time to adjust to market forces.

Another goal is protection of intellectual property
rights, for example, patent protection for phar-
maceuticals and chemicals, copyright protection
for sound recordings and computer software,
trade secret protection for manufacturing pro-
cesses and data, effective enforcement against
trademark and product counterfeiting, and effective enforcement against the piracy of copyright-
ed materials, such as books, motion pictures, and
recordings.

The United States also wants GATT to ensure that
international rules of fair play cover services. Insurance companies, travel agencies, and other
service firms must be able to set up shop in foreign countries and be treated like local firms.

Another U. S. goal is for GATT to end restrictions
on foreign investment. Auto makers, equipment
manufacturers—companies of all kinds—
should be able to invest in foreign countries

without being forced into local partnerships and export or local content requirements.

These are just the highlights, but they illustrate how the U. S. goals for the Uruguay Round negotiations are designed to clear away the barriers to a truly worldwide free enterprise system in the next century. Ambassador Hills has appropriately described that system as one where "entrepreneurs, not government bureaucrats, determine how industries and farms compete and how nations trade."

These are times of volatility and change. Times when high emotions and high expectations provide a vision of what lies ahead. I see the picture of 300,000 East Germans marching through the streets of Leipzig chanting "We are the people," reminding us all that it *is* indeed the drive of the human spirit that motivates freedom and ultimately ensures economic success.

And, so, indeed, the future of the free enterprise system looks bright to me. But it must be a future in which a responsible private sector is willing to share the burdens of protecting the environment and helping the economically underdeveloped societies of the world. It must be a future in which all nations participate in creating a fair and equitable trading system—one that guarantees access to markets and protects the commercial rights of entrepreneurs. And, finally, there must be a healthy United States, with a strong base of globally competitive private enterprise.

We at Procter & Gamble will do our best to do our part—I can guarantee you that.

MORAL AND ETHICAL VALUES
WITHIN THE U. S. ECONOMIC SYSTEM
IN A GLOBAL CONTEXT

by

Jon Lovelace

Jon Lovelace

Jon Lovelace is Chairman of the Board of Capital Research & Management Company and is Vice Chairman and Director of The Capital Group, Inc. He is Chairman of the Board and Director of the Investment Company of America, American Mutual Fund, and Capital Income Builder; President and a Trustee of EuroPacific Growth Fund; and Director of New Perspective Fund—all of which are mutual funds managed by Capital Research & Management Company. He has been with the Capital organization since 1951, at which time the assets managed were less than $50 million. The aggregate of Capital Group companies now manages in excess of $30 billion.

A graduate of Princeton University in 1950 with an A.B. in Economics, Mr. Lovelace received an Honorary Doctor of Laws degree from Claremont McKenna College in 1976, where he is on the Board of Trustees and served as Chairman from 1973 to 1976.

Mr. Lovelace's other professional, civic, and cultural associations include serving as a Trustee and former Chairman of the Board of California Institute of the Arts; a member of the Board of Fellows of Claremont University Center; Chairman of the Board of Trustees of the J. Paul Getty Trust; a Director of American Public Radio, Inc.; a Trustee of the Santa Barbara Medical Foundation Clinic; a member of the Advisory Council of the Stanford University Graduate School of Business; a member of the Advisory Board for the Northeast Asia-U. S. Forum on International Policy at Stanford University; a member of the Council on Foreign Relations; and a life member of the Sierra Club.

MORAL AND ETHICAL VALUES WITHIN THE U. S. ECONOMIC SYSTEM IN A GLOBAL CONTEXT

by

Jon Lovelace

That is really quite a tongue twister of a title! Let me describe how it came about.

I was honored to be asked to deliver one of this year's Andrew R. Cecil Lectures on Moral Values in a Free Society. The particular theme for 1989 is: "Our Economic System: Its Strengths and Weaknesses." In my comments, I wanted to give particular emphasis to the global context for this theme—it seems important to consider how the increasing interdependence of the world economies impacts our economic system and its ethical values.

In approaching this topic, I would like to start with my own assessment of how moral and/or ethical values are affecting and influencing the functioning of the U. S. economic system today. Then we can take a look at which of our system's strengths and/or weaknesses are accentuated by increasing global involvement, competition, and cooperation. In addition, we can contemplate the implication and potential consequences of the development of transnational and/or multicultural organizations. Finally, I would like to talk about four specific subjects:

(1) U. S./Japan trade conflicts in relation to the underlying value systems of the two countries;

(2) Securities trading, worldwide and around-the-clock.

(3) The recent surge in take-over and buy-out ac-
     tivities within the U. S. economic system—
     and the dilemma of the ethical institutional
     investor;

(4) The increasing awareness of, and sensitivity
     to, environmental and ecological issues, and
     the consequent impact on the U. S. and other
     economies.

The Influence of Moral Values on the U. S. Economy

A dramatic increase in the attention given to corporate codes of ethics has been taking place over the
last 15 years. Before that time, there were numerous
company "creeds," but the large number of codes introduced in the 1970s was most probably the result
of the investigation of foreign and domestic bribery
by leading corporations, discovered in 1973–1976
by the Securities and Exchange Commission, the
Department of Justice, and the Internal Revenue
Service. (Dr. George C. S. Benson, "Codes of Ethics,"
address delivered at Henry Salvatori Center, Claremont McKenna College, 1989.)

In addition to imposing strict limitations on commercial or political bribery, most codes forbid conflicts of interest and attempt to prescribe rules for
relations on the part of employees with customers
or clients or with the general public. Relationships
within the organization receive some attention but
less frequently than other topics.

Not surprisingly, the codes can vary significantly
in their areas of emphasis. There is also undoubtedly

some considerable variation in the degree to which these codes are supported and emphasized by a company's management and genuinely integrated into the "corporate culture." Furthermore, there appears to be a sharp increase in the number of private foundations, or "centers" at educational institutions, devoted primarily or importantly to corporate and governmental ethical issues.

Despite this increased attention being accorded to matters of ethics, every week seems to bring new stories about overt fraud, in addition to allegations of questionable ethical practices. Saul W. Gellerman, writing in the *Harvard Business Review*, provides a set of explanations as to how ethical misbehavior can take place in organizations, even where there is a stated ethical code:

> "In my view, the explanations go back to four rationalizations that people have relied on through the ages to justify questionable conduct: believing that the activity is not 'really' illegal or immoral; that it is in the individual's or the corporation's best interest; that it will never be found out; or that because it helps the company the company will condone it. By looking at these rationalizations, we can develop some practical rules to more effectively control managers' actions that lead to trouble—control, but not eliminate. For the hard truth is that corporate misconduct, like the lowly cockroach, is a plague that we can suppress but never exterminate." (Gellerman, "Why 'Good' Managers Make Bad Ethical Choices," 64 *Harvard Business Review*, July/Aug. 1986, p. 85.)

Furthermore, some of our well-intentioned solutions to one set of problems have, in turn, created new and unforeseen consequences and new opportunities for the fraudulent—there are certainly a number of examples in the savings and loan industry in Texas and California alone to make this point.

So what we have is an increased emphasis on moral values primarily on the part of established companies and industry leaders, while at the same time there seems little diminution in the magnitude of legal and moral transgressions.

I hold the belief that an individual's or a company's or a nation's *strength* often has a concurrent "dark" side, so that the strength also represents a weakness, an area of vulnerability. Our carefully developed legal system serves to provide the definition of which violations of our moral and ethical standards are to be considered illegal and subject to punishment. We have an elaborate structure of laws and an extensive procedure to attempt to assure a fair and consistent interpretation of these laws. But, as one consequence, these laws and procedures can lead to the primary question in a corporation being, "Is it legal?" with much less frequent focus on the question, "Is it ethical?"

Another consequence is that the basic focus of attention is on the transgressor and on his (or her or their) punishment. It is regrettable that almost all the attention is on the negative in matters of business ethics. An important recent step in this regard has been the recent formation of the Business Enterprise Trust, which is described as follows:

"The Business Enterprise Trust is a new national organization dedicated to identifying and promoting acts of courage, integrity and social vision which exemplify the highest standards of business responsibility. The Trust was founded in 1989 by seventeen prominent leaders in American business, academia, labor and the media.

"Through its annual awards program, panel studies, research projects, publications and symposia, the Trust seeks to stimulate a national debate on responsible business behavior in the complex new economy of the 1990s and beyond.

"The trustees believe that a strong, competitive private enterprise system has been the foundation of our national economic prosperity and the cornerstone of our personal and political liberty. Today, however, many Americans, including some in business, believe that pressures in the marketplace and inside the corporation make it more difficult for business to behave in ways that serve the common good and exhibit courage, integrity and social vision.

"Through careful inquiry and research, the Trust will determine how business leaders can [respond] and have responded in creative, morally thoughtful ways to the complex and changing business environment; how they have overcome complicated pressures for short-term performance to address vital long-term concerns of both business and society; and how they have demonstrated courageous and principled behavior in critical business situations. The Trust seeks to

shine a spotlight on such acts of business responsibility."

In today's complex society, corporate managers
face a wide array of demands and expectations. I am
indebted to Elliot Richardson for the following bril-
liantly succinct sentence summarizing many of those
things for which a corporate chief executive is held
accountable by society:

> "We, the people, expect you, the managers of your
> company, to provide to us the highest quality
> product at the lowest possible price, produced un-
> der conditions of maximum safety to the worker,
> [and] minimal impact on the environment, while
> conserving energy and generating the capital
> necessary to put constantly increasing numbers
> of people to work at ever higher standards of
> living."

Quite clearly, it is very difficult or impossible for any
corporate manager to meet all these demands simul-
taneously. In most instances the best one can realistically expect is balanced attention to each over time.

While Elliot Richardson's summary does provide
a reasonably comprehensive listing of the primary
areas of "accountability" for a manager, the above-
mentioned differences in what various segments of
"we the people" consider important presents a particular challenge. We do not have a homogeneous
"value system" in the United States. As a result, different segments of our populace emphasize different

aspects of this charge. Therefore, if any part of this listing is ignored, one can rest assured that those outside the organization who consider that particular aspect to be of paramount importance will find ways to call public attention to the failure. The challenge is even greater for companies operating multinationally, since the emphasis on what "we the people" (and, in a number of instances, "we the government") want can vary importantly in different cultures.

Toward a Globalized Economy

The history of the increased "globalization" of the world's markets is interesting. For centuries the primary pattern was a combination of domestic market plus export business. Some companies were well established in certain overseas markets, particularly when these were part of colonial empires; but, in the main, it was domestic plus export. The concept of multinational companies really began to flourish for the United States after World War II, and particularly in the 1960s. Still, the pattern structurally within most U. S. companies was to divide their business into "domestic" and "international" (or "overseas") operations.

During the 1980s, a new pattern began to emerge. One term that has been used to refer to this pattern is "the multicultural corporation." As Robert J. Samuelson has argued in *The Washington Post*, the large multinational corporations are beginning to lose their national identities.

"Of course, big companies have long been global.

In 1988, U. S. companies had $327 billion invest-
ed abroad and about 6 million overseas workers.
But most multinational companies have never fit
the stereotype of truly stateless enterprises. They
have retained their national character. After
World War II, U. S. companies invested in foreign
markets on the basis of superior technology and
products. American companies could make and
sell abroad what they had perfected in the United States.

"What this meant is that overseas operations
tended to remain separate from and subordinate
to U. S. corporate headquarters. In different ways,
the same has been true of Japanese and European multinational firms. For example, the Japanese
advantage lay primarily in superior manufacturing. Costs were low, quality high. So Japanese
companies manufactured at home and created
huge sales companies abroad. But control remained firmly in Japan.

"It is this reality that's now quietly changing.
Companies are increasingly disregarding national
boundaries and trying to organize their manufacturing, product development and research on a
genuinely worldwide basis." (Robert J. Samuelson,
"The Multicultural Corporation: Globalization in
Industry," *The Washington Post*, Aug. 23, 1989,
p. A 27, col. 1.)

Samuelson notes that the formulas that corporations have relied on for decades to provide overseas
expansion no longer work. U. S. companies no
longer have a monopoly on advanced technology,

and Japanese companies are no longer able simply to manufacture at home and sell abroad, since protectionist measures by other nations and higher exchange rates for the yen are forcing Japanese companies to build manufacturing plants elsewhere.

In making his point about the globalization of corporations, Samuelson cites a book by Christopher A. Bartlett and Sumantra Ghoshal (*Managing Across Borders: The Transnational Solution*, Harvard Business School, 1989) that argues that the terms of competition are changing. The success or failure of companies will increasingly depend on how well they adapt themselves and become truly multicultural organizations.

"American companies have some advantages. English is the global business language, and Americans are generally accepting of outsiders. But many American executives dislike working abroad. . . . Japanese strengths and weaknesses are reversed. Executives go abroad in great numbers, but Japanese companies have a reputation for keeping non-Japanese from positions of power. Bartlett thinks European firms—with a cosmopolitan tradition—may do best at the cultural balancing act.

"What it means for our national well-being is simple enough. The marketplace for ideas and technologies is now worldwide. Companies are the means of transmission. The nations that prosper will be those best able to exploit the best new ideas and technologies—whatever their origin." (*Ibid.*)

Another description of this developing business form is the "transnational" corporation—one that truly has *no* national base. To my mind, the term "multicultural" can apply to a U. S. or Japanese or European multinational and has many positive aspects. But I think there are questions as to whom a "transnational" is ultimately responsible, in addition to its owners.

The Economic Implications of Cultural Differences Between Japan and the United States

People in all countries will have to learn much about one another before corporations can truly arrive at being multicultural. An inevitable consequence of increased economic activity between and among countries is the likelihood of misunderstandings and conflicts based upon different cultural attitudes regarding what is fair. This problem is superimposed upon what I would consider the normal bureaucratic and industrial attempts to protect home markets, while trying to exploit foreign opportunities as fully as possible.

While numerous examples of such problems exist around the world, I find the U. S.-Japan trade conflicts to be particularly significant because these two countries are such a major part of the world economic scene and the consequences of severe policy conflicts could be so great. I would assume that all of you have a general awareness of many of these issues, and some of you know particular aspects in considerable detail. Suffice it to say that many Americans resent what they perceive as Japan's closed markets, while, they feel, Japanese companies have had full opportunity to take advantage of our open economic system. This feeling is summed up in the concept that what is needed is "fair trade, not just free trade."

At this point, however, an unexpected difficulty arises. As we have not always understood sufficiently, the notion of "fairness" may not always be one that transcends national and cultural boundaries. It was interesting in this regard for me to read recently a paper written by Jun-Ichi Hattori of Seiko in Japan, subsequent to his having participated in the Eisenhower Exchange Fellowship Program. Hattori points out that American frustrations arise from the fact that the Japanese policymaking system and market mechanism are opaque from the outside. We in the United States can neither see nor understand how these decisions are being made, whereas U. S. policymaking is more or less visible and intelligible to people in other countries. This contrast has created a fundamental problem, in that Americans have begun to believe that the Japanese process is unfair.

Hattori believes that a dialogue about these issues that might arrive at mutual understanding is extremely difficult because our differences with one another go much deeper. He contends that "the concept of fairness is very much intrinsic to a country's unique, individual cultural and historical background" and points out that the United States and Japan operate under entirely different assumptions as to what constitutes fairness. The U. S., as a nation of immigrants, has constructed a decentralized social and governmental system where no individual or group is invested with great power. Strong

government is distrusted. A society composed of people from many different cultural and ethnic back-
grounds has had to lay out basic social rules as clearly
as possible so as to avoid misunderstandings. There
is thus a strong emphasis on due process of law, and
the idea of fairness is bound up in such a process.
A legal dispute is regarded as having been decided
fairly—even when the outcome is not satisfactory for
each individual—as long as the legal process is fair.

According to Hattori's account, the Japanese social system operates out of quite different expectations and assumptions:

> "Japan is a country of a long history and tradi-
> tion. Despite the country's long history, the
> Japanese have never experienced a major civil
> war. However, Japan has experienced internal
> conflicts; there have always been wars between the
> aristocratic military, samurai soldiers, but they
> were a far cry from civil war. Throughout Japa-
> nese history, particularly during the 350 years of
> the Tokugawa shogunate era, Japan had a strong
> autocratic government and enjoyed peace and
> economic prosperity throughout that period.
> Therefore, Japanese are traditionally pro strong
> government. They trust a single consistent pow-
> er structure to control and sustain their society.
> "It is typical in Japan that when there is a dis-
> agreement, consensus building is generally cho-
> sen over fighting through a legal process. Since
> Japan is basically a homogeneous society, people
> share more or less the same cultural background
> and value system, thus consensus building is more

efficient and certainly less time consuming. However, the consensus building procedure is totally
opaque from the outside by nature, simply
because if you open up the argument, you would
invite more participants and hence, it would become more difficult to reach a mutually acceptable consensus."

I find Hattori's summary of Japanese expectations
interesting and concise:

"In addition to being opaque, a consensus building system tends to be result-oriented, because
participants seek to share a gain or burden among
themselves at some mutually acceptable level.
"Therefore, the Japanese do not concentrate
much on the actual problem solving process, so
long as the outcome is somewhat acceptable and
fair to the parties involved. In other words, what
is fair to the Japanese is to seek a fair outcome
among the participants."

Stemming importantly from these cultural differences are the areas in which we criticize each other.
Americans feel that Japanese business does not treat
its Japanese customers fairly and in the process uses
high domestic prices to subsidize sales in the U. S.
market. We criticize Japan for not being as open to
"shareholder rights" as is the case in our country
(although, in my opinion, their practices also permit
Japanese companies to take a longer-term view). Furthermore, we often point out the discriminatory situation female employees face in much of Japanese
industry.

In turn, the Japanese criticize what they see as our overemphasis on consumerism and our low personal savings rate. With a cultural pattern of "lifetime employment," they question many of our employment practices. They also see us as self-indulgent and lazy, blaming others for things we should be correcting ourselves. One catch phrase is, "We in Japan work for the future; you work for the weekend."

I want to cite two other illustrations of Japanese practices as opposed to American ones because I think they help illustrate differences between what is perceived as fair and ethical behavior in the two countries. The first example relates to airline pricing. Hattori asks a U. S. executive:

> "Why should you be charged more to fly from Los Angeles to Dayton, Ohio, than to fly from Los Angeles to New York? Is this something that's considered to be fair? His [the executive's] argument was . . . very logical. He said because there are more passengers who fly from LA to NYC, the airline can use a larger fleet with consistently high occupancy, which allows them to lower overhead costs. Therefore, the airlines are able to charge less. Even though the process of calculating airline ticket prices seems fair, most Japanese would not consider this fair."

Hattori points out that

> "many people move from the countryside to a major city in pursuit of a better job, both in

America and Japan. In Japan, traditionally those city workers go back to their local home town twice a year, for New Year's Day and for the summer Buddhist festival—to spend those festive occasions together with their extended family: grandparents, parents, and aged relatives. If an individual was charged more to go back to his home town, Sendai, a few hours to the north, than a person who goes back to Hokkaido, the northernmost island in Japan, he would not accept it. No matter how you explain it logically, he would assume that the opportunity should be equally fair among the people to spend these occasions in their home town. Again, this illustrates the differences on the concept of fairness between Japanese and Americans."

Hattori also describes the different attitudes toward negotiations in the two countries. When the United States and Japan were negotiating the matter of semiconductors, for instance, the Japanese wanted to keep the binding terms of the agreement to a minimum in the hope that this would improve the flexibility needed to achieve the desired goals. The United States, however, expected the negotiations to achieve clearly binding legal terms—once again, they wanted to be assured that the *process* was fair. The result, sadly, was that the two countries eventually found that they had different understandings of the agreement, and the first reaction of the Americans was to feel that they had been deceived by the Japanese.

Hattori's analysis of the respective weaknesses of

the cultural assumptions of each of our two nations is acute:

> "Sometimes the strict legalism of the U. S. prevents them from adjusting their policy implementation to respond to the rapidly changing business environment, and eventually leads them to unintended results. While, on the other hand, the Japanese predilection for respecting pragmatism over legalism is certainly dangerous when Japan lacks strong government discipline. Of course, no system can be completely perfect."

I agree with Jun-Ichi Hattori that there is a great need for opening avenues of communication between the United States and Japan, because as of yet we do not have the deep mutual understanding, at both social and cultural levels, that is so vital to our relationship. Our cultures are sufficiently different that bridging the gap will be a complex process, and it will take time. But, as Hattori says, "It is essential for us to continue forging ahead to build a mutual understanding between our countries. It may be the most important responsibility we will ever face."

The U.S.-Japanese relationship that I have been discussing provides a useful perspective in evaluating the American economic system in its global setting. Seeing how different countries can perceive a value such as fairness in such contradictory ways is only one illustration of our need to grow in mutual understanding and respect.

Securities Trading: Worldwide and Around-the-Clock

The topic of securities trading is highly timely and offers a dramatic example of rapid globalization. Throughout most of this century, transactions in stocks and bonds have taken place through securities dealers, on stock exchanges, or in so-called over-the-counter markets. In the United States, the New York Stock Exchange has been the primary market, followed by the American Stock Exchange, formerly called the Curb. In many other countries, there is one primary market, such as in London or in Paris; in some, such as Australia or Germany, there are two or more. Another set of markets around the world trades in commodities and commodity futures.

Whatever the location of the market or the characteristics of the financial instrument being traded, several generalizations can be made:

(1)   A great deal of opportunity exists for ethical abuse by taking advantage of financial opportunities or by preventing financial loss.

(2)   As a result, self-regulatory bodies have been formed to maintain standards and to enforce rules. Some of these have worked well, some have not.

(3)   Where things have not worked well, some nations have followed the approach of setting up governmental regulatory bodies.

During the 1960s and 1970s, the number of multinational companies that chose to have their shares listed and traded on foreign exchanges, in addition to their home market, increased, and a number of

securities firms sought and attained rights of membership to trade on foreign exchanges, in addition
to their domestic membership. In the course of this
latter trend, the self-regulatory exchange bodies,
which had often been quite "clubby" in nature, found
it necessary to amend their ways of rule setting.

The 1980s brought revolutionary change, the consequences of which we have yet to see. Four aspects
seem to me of major importance:

(1) Technological developments now make infor-
     mation and data, accurate or not, available
     almost instantaneously around the world.

(2) Over just a few years, the capability has devel-
     oped to trade securities essentially around-
     the-clock, through the electronic linking of
     national markets around the world.

(3) New financial instruments, sometimes termed
     "synthetic securities," have proliferated. No
     longer does a buyer focus just on the stocks
     and bonds of specific companies or on future
     contracts of specific commodities. Now we
     have stock index futures that treat a "basket
     of stocks" as a commodity. This "basket" then
     links back to the prices of the individual
     stocks that make up the basket, and, through
     "program trading," a change in the group
     price can cause the individual prices to move
     sharply, up or down, in unison.

(4) The national and local regulatory bodies
     operate much as they did before all these
     changes took place.

I would conclude with one simple but disturbing
thesis: I think it highly probable that somewhere in

this world one or more unethical entrepreneurs have hit upon a way to commit systematic fraud upon this newly developed and highly technological, inadequately overseen global trading system and that this fraud involves large financial stakes. If we the people, or any of the regulators, could anticipate or know the specific operating methods of such a scheme, we would initiate steps to prevent it. But, unfortunately, we do not. I expect that we will find out that some such fraud has occurred, and then regulatory oversight will follow.

Corporate Takeovers and the Institutional Investor

Before turning to the important subject of corporate takeovers and buy-outs, and the dilemma of the ethical institutional investor, first let me make some brief comments about the investment management organization with which I am affiliated, the Capital Group. We are primarily institutional money managers, with various Capital Group companies managing mutual funds, pension funds, and endowment funds, plus a limited number of larger individual accounts. Our investment approach is "fundamental" in nature, which means we try to get to know well the managements of companies, the nature of their businesses, the strategies being used, etc. We then evaluate the likelihood of success, plus the degree to which this likelihood is being discounted in the market, for the various companies in which we are interested.

I will give you a little story that illustrates some of the cultural differences that can pertain to such "fundamental" investing. At a client meeting a few years ago in Europe, one of my associates was sitting in the audience as another associate was talking about this fundamental approach, our emphasis on basic investment research, really getting to know companies well, investing for the long term, and not trading on inside information. Seated in back of my associate were several European investors, one of whom whispered to the other, "Frankly, I prefer inside information."

We are long term in orientation, with relatively low turnover both in our investment portfolios and in the personnel in our organization. Over more than three decades we have been able to generate consistently above-average investment results. This contrasts with frequent articles in the press and in financial publications that institutional investors do not "beat the averages" over time. That may be valid in the aggregate, but a number of firms are consistently superior over time, and we are one of them.

As long-term investors, we encounter problems (1) in terms of proxy issues and (2) on occasions when there is an attempt to take over or buy out a company. Since we normally have invested in companies we like, we tend to vote with management on most issues.

In the 1980s, however, there has been a dramatic increase in the number of proposed hostile takeovers. When there is a takeover proposal, the stock goes up sharply. As institutional investors, we are employed by our clients to produce investment results, so there is then pressure on us to vote in a way that will achieve this higher price. This comes about because most clients focus very heavily on recent results. Institutional investors also face the consequence that if the takeover offer does not succeed, it is likely that the price of the stock will go down again. A very good recent example of a takeover offering a sharp price markup and a quick return is United Airlines.

In some instances, the company that is the target of the takeover seems to us to be well managed and to have a good long-term future. Yet, by selling out at the higher price, we can get a handsome financial return for our client. The problem is that one loses the opportunity to invest in that management and that company over the longer time period; yet, if one votes against the proposal, one risks a price loss, and many clients would much rather take advantage of the short-term opportunity.

There is a great irony here, because many corporate executives criticize the institutional investor for taking this shorter-term view. Yet, if they look at ways in which their own corporate pension funds are administered, they may find that their own funds are administered in a way that rewards this very behavior.

As I have said, we have a longer-term view, and this outlook is reflected in some of our votes and some of our actions. If a good company is, in our opinion, being operated well over time, and we would like to be able to continue to have the opportunity to invest in that company, we have on a number of occasions taken that long-term view in our vote. The difficulty is that that can cause negative shorter-term results and impact shorter-term comparisons. It is a very difficult issue the way the system is structured now, because all the pressures are toward the short-term realization of higher prices.

I do not have an easy answer to this problem. We have the advantage in our case that our clients know that we are longer-term oriented. We have stated our views, and we are well enough established that we can afford to follow this approach with less penalty than a newer organization might face. But, even for us, it is never easy to make such a decision and to make our case to our clients. I think this is one of the most difficult issues that our society faces.

Those who favor the present trend say that many companies are inefficiently run and that, because of this wave of takeovers during the last decade, the efficiency of American business is being improved. In some instances there is merit to this argument. Against this trend, however, is the impact on American industry of an increasingly shorter-term focus. Another problem of the takeover trend has been an increase in economic risk because of the financial leverage that is involved. The overall consequence of a shorter-term focus and increased leverage is that, as a nation, we may be reducing our effectiveness in global competition.

Awareness of the Environment

The fourth specific area I would like to cover relates to the increasing awareness of, and sensitivity to, environmental and ecological issues and the impact of this on the U. S. and other economies. You are familiar with many of the problems and questions. These include, in no particular order,

Air pollution
Water pollution—oceans, lakes, rivers
Acid rain
The ozone layer
Global warming and the "greenhouse effect"
Global cooling
Toxic waste disposal
The advantages and risks of nuclear energy
Wilderness preservation
Endangered species and wildlife protection
Tropical rain forest destruction
Reforestation needs and the preservation of the
  redwoods
Oil spills
Energy conservation
Declining water tables
Impact of pesticides on foods
The silting behind dams

Concerns about matters such as these arise because
of many reasons, including

A variety of health issues
Worries about future resource availability—
  energy, water, etc.
"Quality of life"
Wilderness needs—for recreation, for "the
  balance of nature"
The well-being of future generations
Survival of the planet

Some potential economic consequences are

Reduction in natural resources available for
current commercial use
Higher consumer costs for many products
Reduced employment in certain fields
Increased governmental expenses and higher
taxes

These consequences may be offset, at least in part,
by business and employment opportunities relating
to solutions to some of these problems.

The moral issues involved include

Obligations to future generations
Present gratification versus the needs of *current*
generations a bit later in their life
Responsibility for the impact on others of one's
own acts

To my mind, the mutual relationship of the environment and the economy is perhaps the most all-
encompassing, complicated issue we face. It is *truly*
global in scope. It has an impact on economic, political, and health matters in almost every country,
and the different value systems of different cultures
will lead to different priorities. The nature of the
risks of error are generally nonquantifiable, conjec-
tural, and debatable. Current desires need to be
balanced against perceived future needs. These considerations lead me to believe that this broad topic
could be a candidate for a future theme for this lecture series, much like the topic "Traditional Moral
Values in the Age of Technology" in 1986.

In prior centuries and in ancient cultures, nature was a subject of reverence and awe. In recent decades, the attitude has shifted to one of "conquering" nature, "controlling" nature, "harnessing" nature. Perhaps in the future we can work toward a more tangible and intangible partnership, benefiting from many of the fruits of our natural environment but also loving it, respecting its ecological complexities, and, where possible, aiding and giving back to it.

In conclusion, I shall not attempt a summary but rather will emphasize two particular points about the strengths and weaknesses of our economic system. I believe that the greatest weakness of the U. S. economic system over recent years has been our increasingly short-term focus. There are many causes. This characteristic seems to pervade many aspects of our culture. The risky consequence is that we are borrowing from, or mortgaging, our longer-term future. It is something we can change. The question is whether we have the will to do so.

I believe that the greatest strength of our economic system is the ways we have found, over the decades, to make possible the utilization of individual initiative, imagination, creativity, and hard work. As our economy becomes larger, more complex, and more globally integrated, it is essential that we maintain this individualism. It is also essential, however, that this individualism have a foundation of moral and ethical values, and a sense of social responsibility, to help assure that this creativity is used constructively. To that end, these Andrew R. Cecil Lectures make an important contribution.

ETHICS AND CORPORATE GOVERNANCE IN THE AGE OF PENSION FUND CAPITALISM

by

Elmer W. Johnson

Elmer W. Johnson

Elmer W. Johnson is a partner in the Chicago office of Kirkland & Ellis. He joined the firm in 1956, became a partner in 1962, and has been a member of the firm's managing committee since 1971.

From 1981 to 1983, Mr. Johnson served as General Counsel for International Harvester Company during its reorganization, and in 1982-83 he served as Special Counsel to the Chairman of Ameritech Corporation in connection with the breakup of AT&T. From May 1, 1983, to June 30, 1988, he held various offices at General Motors Corporation, with responsibility during all or most of that period for the Legal, Operating, and Public Affairs staffs. In May 1987, he was elected Executive Vice President and a director of the Company and served as a member of the Executive and Finance Committees of the Board. On July 1, 1988, he retired from General Motors and returned to the full-time private practice of law at Kirkland & Ellis.

Mr. Johnson is a Trustee of the University of Chicago and the Aspen Institute, and he serves on the Legal Advisory Committee to the New York Stock Exchange. Because of Mr. Johnson's lecturing and writing on ethics and economic organization, he has been awarded various honorary degrees, and in 1989 he was elected as a Fellow of the American Academy of Arts and Sciences.

Born in Denver, Colorado, on May 2, 1932, Mr. Johnson received a B.A. from Yale University in 1954 and a J.D. from the University of Chicago Law School in 1957.

ETHICS AND CORPORATE GOVERNANCE IN THE AGE OF PENSION FUND CAPITALISM

by

Elmer W. Johnson

History may well record that our generation, more than any other in our nation's past, cashed in on the legacy of its ancestors and mortgaged its grandchildren's future. This judgment would certainly seem to apply to our exploitation of the environment, our failure to maintain societal infrastructures, and our incurrence of massive government debt to benefit the living at the expense of the unborn. My remarks can be viewed as a consideration of this broad issue of fairness between generations as it pertains to the governance of the large business corporation.

My thesis is that the large public corporation, under the governance of an independent board of directors, is one of the most remarkable organizational achievements of this century; that its high purpose is to serve society as an intergenerational, wealth-creating institution, recognizing that it takes decades to build the creative work environment and the capital base that enable people with complementary talents to thrive and unleash their productive energies; that, in general, the public corporation in the United States served its purposes rather well for decades but that since the mid-1960s the cracks have begun to show; and that the public corporation is now an endangered species and we must take strong measures to preserve and renew it.

This then is the subject matter of my talk. In my paradigm, the public corporation relies for its legitimacy on the proper functioning of the board of directors, which is the precondition to the provision of patient capital, and patient capital in turn is the foundation for the building of long-term wealth-creating institutions. The providers of patient capital understand that their managers must enter into long-term, usually implicit, compacts with employees, suppliers, and communities and that these compacts spawn the relationships of mutual trust and cooperation by which the productive potential of the organization is realized. But, of course, patient capital is helpless capital unless it can exercise a strong voice. Managers can fail and need replacing. Also, the top personnel needs of even a mature enterprise can change over time. Thus, without boards of directors who have the courage and fiduciary conscience to monitor management, there can be no such thing as a public corporation geared to the long-term goals of creating jobs and wealth.

Along with other legal commentators, I see capitalism as an evolving process. In the first few decades of this century, we evolved from a market society dominated by corporations whose managers owned the controlling stock to one dominated by corporations with absentee owners and hired professional managers. Adam Smith, and later Adolf A. Berle, Jr., and Gardiner C. Means, doubted that capitalism could continue to flourish in an era of absentee stock ownership. Yet, despite their concerns, we developed a market order during the middle third of this century in which the large, professionally managed corporation had come to play the principal role and in which the corporate managers were expected to act primarily not out of self-interest but as fiduciaries.

If Adam Smith had risen from his grave and paid a visit to our country in the late 1950s, he would have been staggered by the economic miracle we had wrought and by the tolerable working order of the fiduciary ethic that (among other conditions) made this miracle possible. The success of managerial capitalism can be attributed in part to the evolution of corporate and securities laws governing responsibilities of managers to investors, in part to the business schools for bringing about the professionalization of management, in part to the introduction of compensation and incentive arrangements that work to align the corporate interest and the manager's self-interest. In these and other ways, we were able to minimize Smith's and Berle and Means's concerns over managerial capitalism.

Yet, by the 1960s the cracks were beginning to show, and 25 years later, the symptoms of ill health had become rather serious. This is the story to which I now turn.

Joseph Schumpeter, the famous economist, said that the very genius and essence of capitalism is its relentless process of "creative destruction." But, as we look back on the period from the end of World War II to about 1973, it almost seemed then that U. S. industry was exempt from Schumpeter's cruel law. Given the conditions of war-torn Europe and Japan, the United States quickly came to dominate commerce and trade in the free world. During this unusual period of stability and prosperity, corporate cultures grew ever more bureaucratic and rigid, top management often tended to become more remote from operations, and boards became more passive.

The Growth of Bureaucratic Cultures

Within such cultures, few of the middle managers were being groomed for bottom-line responsibility and accountability: that is, to exercise the kind of peripheral vision and integrating judgment required of top managers of operating units. Management responsibility became terribly fragmented and diffuse. These executives did not make, and were not expected to make, the difficult trade-offs involving market, technology, and cost considerations.

Second, the culture discouraged open, frank debate among executives in the pursuit of problem resolution. There existed a clear perception among the rank and file that top management does not receive bad news well.

Third, a strong bias developed toward small distinctions in pay regardless of wide differences in performance. The factor of years of service became the overriding criterion for both promotions and salary increases. As a consequence, managers and workers developed notions of entitlement, cradle-to-grave security, regular raises—in short, the club mentality: "I now belong to the club; if I don't rock the boat and if I keep my nose clean, my remaining years will be quite comfortable." The top young talent could not help but perceive that there was little or no light at the end of the tunnel.

Fourth, the young professional experts—the best brains in the areas of technical expertise that were critical to the corporation's future—were usually forced by their mid-thirties to become managers if they wished to keep climbing the corporate ladder. Then, after five years as managers, they had lost their edge as professionals. The corporation paid a heavy price for failing to provide a separate professional, technical career path into the top executive ranks.

Problems at the Top

In the 1960s and 1970s, a dominant new style of management evolved in the top rungs of many of our large corporations. While authority and responsibility were highly fragmented at the middle and lower levels of management, they were highly centralized at the top. Even minor decisions required top executive approval.

With the development of this strong "control" mentality, and given the stability of the times, top management became highly confident of their ability to predict and control the future. Too often they fell in love with their abstract five-year plans and became insensitive to changing hurdles and moving targets. The plan tended to become the goal itself, to be tucked away until next year's update. As managers pursued their quest for global efficiency and rationalization, they often lost sight of the real key to productivity growth: the tapping of human energy and talent.

Many top executives flitted from job to job, or even from company to company, confident that their financial and managerial skills were of universal application and that the product was a mere detail. Further, as new and proposed government regulations raised ever greater threats to the profitability of corporations, chief executive officers spent more and more of their time in Washington. More generally, the CEO became the man of external affairs: giving speeches, meeting with senators, and making acquisitions. In these circumstances, it is not surprising that he was out of touch with the customer, the product, and the technical leadership of his organization.

Finally, in many cases, managers had feathered their own nests over the years, at the expense of stockholders and to the detriment of employee morale. A recent study by *Business Week* shows that by 1988 the average annual compensation of the 700 highest paid CEOs had jumped to more than $2 million, or 93 times the average pay of a factory worker and 72 times that of a schoolteacher. In 1960, on the average, the 700 top CEOs made only 41 times as much as the average factory worker and 38 times the salary of the average schoolteacher. (Leonard Silk, "Rich and Poor: The Gap Widens," *New York Times*, May 12, 1989, p. C2, col. 1.)

The Growing Passivity of Boards of Directors

As boards grew larger, their meetings became ever more formal, with slide presentations and scripts carefully edited by the chairman. There was little or no time for give and take or for lively discussion of issues. In this atmosphere, the chairmen tended to be the sole mediators between the board and management.

Second, CEOs tended to select their directors with great care. Significant stock ownership was not a requisite for board membership. New directors were groomed and tested. Those who asked embarrassing questions too often or who questioned the CEOs' judgment too openly were screened out from the inner sanctum, i.e., the nominating and compensation committees.

Finally, most boards developed a club ethos. Their social ties became quite close. Such a culture tended to inhibit the monitoring function of the board. Furthermore, the outgoing chairmen often continued to serve on the board after retiring. The outside directors seldom met alone to discuss management issues, and when they did, the retired chairmen's membership on key committees tended to prevent free and open discussion. After all, the new chairman was often handpicked by his predecessor, and the two of them usually stayed in close communication.

Given the boards' modus operandi, it followed that even if the new CEOs understood the need for radical reform, they were up against almost insuperable obstacles, especially if they were career insiders. How could new CEOs suddenly change colors and repudiate their predecessors, the ones who selected them and who still serve on the board and who had selected many of the other members of the board? Unless a clear crisis arose, it would be more imprudent, if not futile, to take on such a sea of troubles.

Perhaps, as a lawyer, my experience over the last 20 years has warped my judgment. Lawyers do not spend a lot of time with companies in which everything is going well. Further, I should point out that I have never worked with a board where there were not at least a few diligent, independent members who did all that could reasonably be expected of them. But the board culture that I have been sketching usually prevented them from achieving a critical mass at the right time—that is, there were seldom a sufficient number of them to make a difference in time of trouble.

These tendencies I have described—toward bureaucratic corporate cultures, toward a detached, control mentality on the part of top management, and toward a club ethos on the part of boards of directors—are largely the product, I believe, of 25 years or more of unusual stability and prosperity in the United States following World War II. They reflect a basic law of nature: Human beings and organizations tend to become fat, dumb, and comfortable in the absence of occasional external shocks to the system.

Fortunately, on balance, it turned out that the conditions of stability and predictability for the post-World War II era were an aberration of history. Schumpeter's law, the law of "creative destruction," holds true in the long run. Over the last 15 years, our large bureaucratic corporations have been shaken to their foundations as a result of a number of powerful new forces that are at work in the world.

The New Forces of Change

One of these forces is the explosion of information technology: the technology of data processing, storage, retrieval, and transmission. The new electronic connections between organizations enable them to gain rapid and equal access to pertinent information and to reduce transaction costs so that large hierarchical organizations no longer enjoy their former long-standing advantage over smaller competitors. Large corporations are thus being forced to consider divestment or decentralization of operations that can be carried out less expensively and more flexibly by autonomous suppliers whose selection and work can be coordinated by computer-based systems.

A second development is the advent of flexible manufacturing technology. Henry Ford's concept of achieving ultimate efficiency and value by producing the maximum number of identical products is obsolete. Today's automated plants can manufacture highly differentiated products on the same assembly line. Let me give you an example. Assuming the optimum-size assembly operation turns out 200,000 cars per year, modern technology enables a manufacturer owning only one plant to turn out perhaps five very distinct models of 40,000 cars each and to compete effectively with a manufacturer owning five plants, each of which is dedicated to producing 200,000 cars of only one model.

Third, the emergence of global markets has enabled formerly small, high-cost producers, such as BMW, to achieve optimum levels of production efficiency by catering to a worldwide market niche. An increasing part of the market is being appropriated by these "boutique" competitors that appeal to the customers' demand for distinctness and are light on their feet in responding to changing technologies and market signals.

Fourth, we have witnessed a moral revolution in the workplace. Traditionally, it was assumed that manufacturing efficiency requires absolute management control over the production process: Management must do all the thinking and decisionmaking; workers carry out orders. Over the last decade, this working assumption has proved to be invalid. We in the United States have had to learn some painful lessons from some of our global competitors: that their competitive advantage lies, not so much in automation or in efficiencies of scale, but primarily in the way the work force is organized and empowered— all the many thoughtful elements designed to elicit the workers' highest contribution and afford them the greatest sense of job satisfaction.

While I do not hold out any of the Japanese or Swedish manufacturing systems as a moral ideal, the best of them have exposed serious flaws in both our institutional mechanisms and our managerial practices pertaining to the mobilization of human resources. It turns out that personal initiative and team play have been grossly underutilized sources of efficiency, sources that are being tapped through a combination of personal accountability and cooperative work arrangements.

Needless to say, the larger and more centralized

the organization, the harder it is to adapt to this moral revolution. It is not easy to observe dignitarian values in a huge, pyramidal organization.

Finally, we have experienced a further profound evolution in corporate capitalism. It consists of the professionalism of the investment function and the emergence of the institutional investor, and this evolution has been accelerated by the increasing importance of forced savings, namely, the growth of pension funds, both public and private. No longer does the average saver decide how to invest his savings in the stock market; he does not even decide how much to save. Companies and unions and governments and educational institutions have pension plans that tell the worker how much of his income will be saved and invested for the future. The administrators then choose the professional investors.

Institutional investors now own more than half the shares listed on the New York Stock Exchange and account for 70 percent of the trading. Since 1960 the annual turnover rate of all that Exchange's listed shares has skyrocketed from 14 percent to 95 percent. That last figure jumps to 200 percent after including trading in options and futures.

Institutional investors trade intensively in index baskets of stock. No particular company matters very much or for very long. Such investors have little or no interest in using the power of *voice* to monitor management. It has not been in the interest of any one holder of a trivial portion (though a large dollar value) of a public company to spend a lot of energy and time prodding or reconstituting boards when the benefits would accrue to free riders. As they say, they prefer the power of *exit*: They vote with their feet. Moreover, institutional investors are measured by how well they perform quarter by quarter against various indices. Then, too, they are playing with other people's money. They have very little personal incentive to make long-term, company-specific invest-ment decisions.

The Impact of the New Forces

I have described several powerful long-term forces that seriously threaten the stability of our large cor-porate behemoths in America. One consequence of these forces is that our largest corporations now have to deal with a new environment of guerilla warfare. General Motors finds that in order to improve its know-how in suspension technology it must buy a tiny British car company called Lotus. IBM must wor-ry mainly about the small Apple Computer compa-nies of this world. The behemoths are in danger of being nibbled to death.

A second consequence is that they must contend with a very different investment climate, one that is dominated by the institutional investor with its short-term focus. Now this short-term investment mentality turns out to be a communicable disease that quickly spreads to management. Over the last decade, the management of almost every widely held corpora-tion, regardless of its excellence and its bias toward long-term institution building, has been required by this new investment climate to look over its shoulder regularly because a takeover artist may be lurking in the shadows. These managements have little choice but to subordinate long-term goals in favor of an all-out effort to report record earnings for each succeeding quarter and to adopt effective anti-takeover measures: poison pills, ingenious charter provisions, and the leveraging of the balance sheet.

Possible Solutions: The Market for Corporate Control

I hope I have convinced you by now that pension fund capitalism is in the midst of a governance crisis. Over the last several years, our market society has been groping for ways to deal with bureaucratic failure, the passivity of boards and institutional investors, and the short-term mentality. Thus far, we have resorted primarily to something called the "junk bond financed leveraged buyout" (the LBO), sometimes initiated by the takeover artist and sometimes by management (in order to avert a takeover). Wall Street and most of academe have strongly supported this tool of the 1980s. Only an unfettered market for corporate control, they argue, will rid our large corporations of entrenched, incompetent management and break monumental bureaucracies down into smaller, more manageable units in which people's energies can be fully tapped. According to Professor Michael Jensen of Harvard Business School, the public corporation is in eclipse:

"The idea that outside directors with little or no equity stake in the company could effectively monitor and discipline the managers who

selected them has proven hollow at best. In practice, only the capital markets have played much
of a control function—and for a long time they
were hampered by legal constraints.

"Indeed, the fact that takeover and LBO premi-
ums average 50% above market price illustrates
how much value public company managers can
destroy before they face a serious threat of dis-
turbance." (Michael C. Jensen, Jay O. Light, and
George F. Baker, Jr., "Eclipse of a Public Corporation," 67 *Harvard Business Review*, Sept.–Oct. 89,
p. 300.)

I agree with much of Professor Jensen's analysis,
but I have mixed emotions about the LBO. It is true
that the LBO has been an effective tool for busting
up bureaucracies and restoring managerial incentives and accountability. Further, as I have tried to
show, economies of scale have been in rapid decline
for the last 15 years, and the restructuring of corporate America must continue. But surely the LBO
cannot serve to replace the public corporation as our
chief mechanism for long-term wealth creation. The
achievement of that goal requires enterprise units
that can adopt and carry out well-considered long-
term strategies.

Alfred Sloan did not build General Motors into a
mighty wealth- and job-creating machine by leveraging the balance sheet and then stripping assets to
service debt. Let me give you an example of how he
did do it. In 1921, Sloan's first year as GM's Chief Executive Officer, Ford had 60 percent of the U. S.

car market and GM had 12 percent. Ford did it with one car, available in one color. GM could not hope to compete on Ford's terms: making the ultimate utilitarian car at the lowest possible cost. Sloan conceived a long-range marketing strategy that called for the creation of "niche" products, a car for every person and purpose. He would nibble away at Ford by giving the public variety and something he called "quality" competition. Thirteen years later, despite many bumps along the way, GM had achieved a 45 percent market share and Ford had been reduced to 20 percent. But, of course, Sloan didn't have to look over his shoulder: Du Pont owned 25 percent of GM. Patient capital, capable management, and a brilliant long-term strategy: an unbeatable combination . . . but one that is most difficult to forge in the current environment.

The LBO creates other adverse side effects. In the 1950s and 1960s, interest payments on corporate debt claimed 16 percent of corporate earnings, leaving the rest for profits and taxes. In the 1970s that figure rose to 33 percent. Today it is close to 60 percent. (Benjamin M. Friedman, *Day of Reckoning*, Random House, 1988, p. 100.) On average, then, a corporation that now earns $100 million per year makes annual interest payments of nearly $60 million, leaving little more than $40 million for profits and taxes. The implications for research, new product development, and mere maintenance of the capital base need hardly be spelled out. Further, while the enormous new leverage may have improved short-term earnings, not in the last 50 years have so many of our corporations been so vulnerable to bankruptcy in the event of a major economic downturn.

Possible Solutions: Revitalizing the Public Corporation

In my judgment, we cannot continue to rely on the LBO as the chief means of reinvigorating our market society. The public corporation remains our best institutional hope. This institution, with its healthy margin of equity, is best able to enter into the compacts and establish the relationships of trust among the various indispensable parties to the task of creating jobs and wealth across generations. This institution has also shown itself best able to maintain the kind of capital structure that enables it to weather the storms and to create and exploit new opportunities. And this institution has shown itself capable of taking the public interest seriously.

Yet, as I have tried to show, the public corporation needs a lot of help. Perhaps the tide is beginning to turn. One spur has been provided by some Delaware court decisions in recent years excoriating directors and their advisers for their lack of diligence and, as one court said, for their "torpid if not supine" conduct in deferring automatically to the CEO in matters where directors should have taken charge. Over the last year or so, a few books and articles have held out some promise that directors are beginning to realize that their main function is to monitor their CEOs, not merely to befriend and counsel them. As John H. Bryan, Jr., Chairman of Sara Lee, recently

put it, the key issue is "the problem of the club
.... You've got to have people with independent
reputations. There is a much greater chance they'll
take on management and defend shareholder interests." (Judith N. Dobrzynski et al., "Taking Charge:
Corporate Directors Start to Flex Their Muscles," *Business Week,* July 3, 1989, p. 70.)

I agree with Mr. Bryan, but I would suggest that
something more is required. First, I sometimes
wonder what would happen to the group dynamic
if boards were limited in size to seven, or nine at
most. Formal slide presentations might suddenly
seem rather inappropriate. An issue-oriented agenda and true deliberation might be difficult to avoid.

Second, we can do much to improve the practices
and procedures of boards of directors so as to further facilitate their monitoring function. For example, it might be appropriate, in the case of certain
large, complex companies where no large stockhold-
ings are represented on the board, for an outside
director to be selected by the board as a sort of om-
budsman. That person's only job would be to con-
sult with the chief executive from time to time on
significant problems facing the company and to
otherwise keep informed about such problems. This
director would have ready access to corporate information and to employees. When a top officer suddenly resigned, the director would routinely conduct
an exit interview. He or she would be expected to
report to the board two or three times a year in the
ordinary course and, in unusual circumstances, to ask
that certain items be placed on the agenda and/or
covered by reports. In the vast majority of instances,
little would ever be required of this director, but his

or her office, with its special duty of inquiry, for which the director would be appropriately compensated, would help to ensure that the board was promptly alerted to potentially serious situations. CEOs of companies in stressful situations are sometimes tempted to filter the information that is provided to directors or to frame the agenda in such a way as to serve the same purpose. This proposal would tend to frustrate any such effort. At the same time, such a mechanism would have to be designed so as to avoid creating unhealthy conditions of distrust.

Third, I believe companies should require their directors, or at least a majority of them, to own a significant number of shares in the company—significant relative to their own personal situations. Besides tending to align their personal interests with the corporate interest, this reform would also serve to limit the number of directorships a person could responsibly assume. Also, companies could devise compensation arrangements for directors under which perhaps half or more of their fees would be in the form of deferred stock payouts.

Fourth, boards of public companies can learn a lot from the LBO experience about how to compensate and motivate top management and put them at risk. Most large corporations dribble out their stock options and bonuses on a yearly basis. The sense of proprietorship that management buyouts foster is a powerful motivation. Managers who become significant owners in the enterprise are often capable of prodigious performance. (B. Charles Ames, "Taking the Risk Out of Leveraged Buyouts," *Wall Street Journal,* Aug. 7, 1989, p. A16, col. 3.)

Fifth, I believe that it is about time that boards of directors assume some responsibility for the overall policy approach respecting the investment of pension monies. Ever since the creation of the Employee Retirement Income Security Act (ERISA) in 1974, boards of directors and their legal counsel, in establishing the apparatus for the administration of corporate pension plans, have been driven chiefly by liability considerations: how to insulate directors and officers from fiduciary liability. As a result, directors abdicated even their ethically nondelegable role of establishing overall direction and purpose. That abdication can no longer be excused in light of the explosion in the size of pension assets and the failure of the investment community to provide a climate conducive to the building of long-term wealth-generating institutions. Legal counsel to boards must become much more imaginative in reasserting the boards' policy role while at the same time protecting boards against undue risk of liability.

Perhaps the money managers would not be so focused on short-term results if boards of directors adopted policies requiring their pension funds to be managed in the long-term interests of the participants, giving due weight to the importance of maintaining an investment climate in which corporations can prosper as long-term wealth-creating institutions. Such policies would reject "go-go" investment strategies intent on maximizing short-term gains in the hope of reducing the corporation's funding obligations and would enunciate an investment policy geared to the long-term responsibility of the company to meet its future payment obligations to retirees in an orderly, risk-averse manner. This purpose, of course, is totally consonant with the concept of patient capital. Its elegant, forceful articulation and implementation could bring about a radical change in the behavior of professional investment advisers and money managers.

Such a policy would surely entail a long-term, company-specific approach to the management of equity portfolios. In Sweden, for example, companies frequently invest a part of their pension funds in large blocks of stock in a handful of companies over which they are able to exert substantial voting control when appropriate. The time is ripe for experimentation, and only time will tell what the wave of the future is. It may become the custom that the large corporation will have a special top-level executive with a small, talented staff that identifies special opportunities for long-term equity investments of very substantial size and voting influence. It may turn out, by some such means, that we restore some old-fashioned accountability on the part of managers and directors.

The old-fashioned way was once evident in this country. I referred earlier to the Du Pont-GM example. Du Pont, owning a substantial block of General Motors stock, simply brought about William Durant's resignation as President in 1920 and the later election of Alfred Sloan to that post. No muss, no fuss, no extraordinary transactional fees to lawyers and bankers, no year-long churning of the market in GM's stock by arbitrageurs, and no aggressive leveraging of GM's capital structure.

Finally, we can also do much to reform the legal and tax framework so as to discourage excessive leverage, to encourage investors to take a longer-term view, and to make it easier for them under the proxy rules to combine forces to prod or reconstitute boards of directors as appropriate.

Please observe that not one of my recommendations calls for the imposition of more liabilities on directors. Too many of my legal brethren have one-track minds: There ought to be yet another law. Rather, most of my recommendations go to structure and practice and style. The law is of very little help in matters of practice and style. The Business Round Table and other prestigious groups should take the lead in advocating governance measures of the kind I have suggested—measures that will enhance the integrity and effectiveness of the board's monitoring function.

I end where I began. The public corporation relies for its legitimacy on the proper functioning of the board of directors. The ability and will of the board of directors to monitor management is the precondition of patient capital and long-term wealth creation. I have proposed a number of structural reforms that I believe would encourage and reinforce the will to monitor. Yet, the most imaginative institutional tinkering in the world will be for naught unless many more directors of our large public corporations muster the courage and the will to conduct themselves with a fiduciary conscience.

In the opening book of *The City of God*, Saint Augustine attempted to explain why God visits his calamities on the good and the evil alike. Saint Augustine's answer was that the Deity was not very impressed with the silence and lack of courage of the so-called good people. Where can we readily find a person, he asked, who has the courage to hold accountable

"those persons on account of whose . . . pride, luxury, and avarice . . . God now smites the earth . . . ? For often we . . . blind ourselves to the occasions of teaching and admonishing them, sometimes of even reprimanding them . . . because we fear to lose good friendships, lest this should stand in the way of our advancement or injure us in some worldly matter, which either our covetous disposition desires to obtain or our weakness shrinks from losing."

Courage is a virtue we do not hear much about nowadays. The other three cardinal virtues— prudence, justice, and self-control—important as they are, seem to me to be of little practical import in the absence of courage. Courage was defined by Plato as the capacity to face unafraid the risk of losing one's life for a worthy cause. I would be happy to witness among the majority of our leaders in the business community a more modest level of courage: the ability to face unafraid the risk of losing a friendship or a material opportunity for the worthy cause of ensuring the legitimacy and competitive vigor of the public corporation.

I have long since concluded that the virtue of

courage is most evident in persons who care deeply about the next generation and about the long-term strength of our important institutions.

CORPORATE GOVERNANCE ISSUES IN THE TAKEOVER ERA

by

J. Edward Fowler

J. Edward Fowler

J. Edward Fowler is currently General Counsel of Mobil Corporation and Mobil Oil Corporation. Prior to assuming his current duties in May 1986, he held a number of legal positions at Mobil which have related primarily to Mobil's international and domestic petroleum business and corporate operations. Before joining Mobil in 1968, Mr. Fowler had spent nine years as a corporate lawyer with the Debevoise & Plimpton law firm in New York City.

Mr. Fowler is a 1953 summa cum laude *graduate of Princeton University, where he was a Politics Department major, a member of Quadrangle Club, and President of the Pre-Law Society. He served in the United States Army during the period 1953-1956 in the United States and Japan. He then attended the Yale Law School, where he was on the Board of Editors of the* Yale Law Journal, *graduating in 1959.*

Mr. Fowler is active in a number of professional associations, including the American Society of International Law, the American Bar Association, the New York State Bar Association, the Association of the Bar of the City of New York, and the Association of General Counsel. Mr. Fowler is a member of the Board of Governors of the American Corporate Counsel Association. He is a member of the Advisory Council of the George Mason University Law School; has been active in Yale Law School alumni affairs, serving as a member of the Executive Committee of the Yale Law School Alumni Association; and is a former President of the Yale Law School Association of New York City. He is currently a member of the Board of Trustees and Chairman of the Development Committee of the American Farm School in Thessaloniki, Greece.

Mr. Fowler has taken an active role in community and civic affairs in his home community of Chappaqua, New York. He served as President of the Chappaqua School Board in 1973, was Moderator of the First Congregational Church of Chappaqua, and later was an Elder of The Presbyterian Church of Mount Kisco. He is former Chairman of the Chappaqua Orchestral Association, which sponsors the Chappaqua Symphony Orchestra.

CORPORATE GOVERNANCE ISSUES
IN THE TAKEOVER ERA
by
J. Edward Fowler

Everyone knows the 1980s have been the era of corporate takeovers in America. We read frequently of
companies, large and small, that are taken over by
someone who either has enough money or is able to
borrow enough money to offer the target shareholders a premium above current market prices. In
many cases the old management is replaced with new
management, and often the company is then dis-
membered and sold off in pieces—sometimes with
substantial reductions in numbers of employees and
dramatic effects on communities where they worked.
Takeover supporters, including many academic experts, claim these events have positive results— improved efficiency, stimulation of more effective
corporate management, and the movement of capital to what they call the highest and best use. Equally prestigious critics in academe and elsewhere
dispute those claims and point to what they believe
are disturbing social and economic dislocations that
result from takeovers and the threat of takeovers.

We shall not resolve that controversy here, or even
try to do so. I shall address, instead, a subject that
is less commonly discussed but is nonetheless linked
to and affected by the takeover phenomenon, namely, the process by which governance of America's business enterprises is determined.

99

Our society has a crucial stake, it seems to me, in the outcome of the corporate governance issues that are in fact being resolved, but not much thought of by the public at large, in the intense activity of the market in the search for corporate control. Who is, or should be, ultimately in charge on decisionmaking for our corporate enterprises and their shareholders? For example, if shareholders want to sell into a tender offer for an immediate short-term profit, should the directors who were elected to serve their interests be allowed to prevent that from happening? In managing a company's business, are directors responsible primarily for enhancing shareholder value by means of short-term measures to support the stock's market price, or should long-term goals of the enterprise be supported for the good of all stakeholders, including affected communities, customers, suppliers, employees, retirees, and the economy as a whole?

What, really, *is* a business corporation? Is it simply a mechanism of shareholder-owners and their controlled managers assigned to serve exclusively the interests, at the time, of those owners? Or is it a more complex social organism of many constituent parts and stakeholders, having a life and purpose of its own? And what of the responsibility of shareholders themselves—especially large institutional investors, who now own more than 50 percent of the stock of America's corporations? Should they assume a duty, or at least be given incentives, to support long-term goals of the enterprise in the face of short-term profit opportunities presented by takeovers? Those are just some of the current issues.

Today's Problems and Yesterday's Analysis

Most of us know that corporate governance issues have been the subject of many writings in the academic literature over the years. I shall suggest, however, that our traditional conceptual approaches and terminology are flawed and are inadequate to the current task. In important respects, they produce overly simplistic answers that address a mythical corporate world that, if it ever existed, has long since disappeared.

Specifically, it seems to me unlikely that useful answers are available by reference to the commonly identified dichotomy of the separation of shareholder "ownership" from managerial "control" or by calling for more or less of something termed "shareholder democracy." Nor do I think society will find that the theorists of the so-called efficient market school of economics, or the work product of their "market for corporate control," will provide answers of sufficient substance and scope.

What we shall point to in this paper is that emerging definitions of managerial responsibility—reflecting input from society but developed in large measure on the initiative of America's corporate managers themselves, as well as that of the courts—are moving toward a reformulation that well suits America's social and economic setting, namely, a concept I will call an "enterprise" theory of corporate governance. This approach asserts that society has an important stake in professional management and long-term investment strategies of its corporate enterprises that take account not only of the long-term interests of shareholders but also the interests of all the other stakeholders of the corporation.

With that brief road map of where we are going, let us touch just briefly on where we have been.

We need not review the history of corporations in the Middle Ages or of the British and Dutch joint-stock companies of the 1600s that were antecedents of the modern business corporation. Suffice it to say that the original concept was that the investors "own" the corporation, its assets, and its business. The investors would then elect directors who as their agents would be responsible for managing the business through officers and managers selected by the directors. While shares typically were transferable, no one could have envisioned a New York Stock Exchange where a global array of strangers to the enterprise would buy and sell millions of "ownership" shares on a daily basis. It was, in the beginning, just assumed that ownership and control would more or less always reside in the same people.

Nonetheless, it was understood as early as 1776, when Adam Smith wrote his famous *Wealth of Nations*, that one attraction of the corporate form was the ability to enlist investment by persons who were strangers to the enterprise and had neither the time nor the interest to concern themselves with conduct of the business. Here is Adam Smith's portrayal of the disinterested stockholder:

"The trade of a joint stock company is always

managed by a court of directors. The court, indeed, is frequently subject, in many respects, to the control of a general court of proprietors. But the greater part of those proprietors seldom pretend to understand anything of the business of the company; and . . . give themselves no trouble about it, but receive contentedly such half yearly or yearly dividend, as the directors think proper to make them. This total exemption from trouble and from risk, beyond a limited sum, encourages many people to become adventurers in joint stock companies, who would, upon no account, hazard their fortunes in any private copartner." (p. 741.)

As time passed, share ownership became more and more dispersed, leaving management of the enterprise more and more in the hands of the directors and their appointed managers. Yet, there seems to have been very little comment over the years to suggest that this was at variance with what investors and society expected or wanted.

In 1932, however, an epochal event occurred: publication of *The Modern Corporation and Private Property* by an economist named Gardiner Means and a Columbia University law professor named Adolf Berle, Jr. That book set both the concepts and the terminology for the next several decades and, to this very day, for debate about corporate governance in America.

In critical tones that reflected the mood of a Depression that was laid by many at the feet of American business, Berle and Means explored in 357

pages the ways in which America's public shareholders, who were viewed historically as the owners
of "private property" consisting of the corporations'
business and assets, had "lost" effective control over
that property. The authors were disturbed by this,
since it seemed at odds with the common-law concept that ownership of property and control of that
property go hand in hand. Reporting what today
would be a quite unsurprising fact, they noted the
broad "dispersion" of public share "ownership" and
contrasted this with the earlier view that a corporate
shareholder is a "quasi-partner, manager and entrepreneur, with definite rights in and to property
used in the enterprise. . . ." (Berle and Means, *The
Modern Corporation and Public Property*, Macmillan,
1962, pp. 278–279.)

   Their book thus exhibited a certain nostalgia for
the idealized American vision of the small, individual
entrepreneur in control of his own destiny. They
said:

> "[I]n the corporate system, the 'owner' of indus-
> trial wealth is left with a mere symbol of owner-
> ship while the power, the responsibility and the
> substance which have been an integral part of
> ownership in the past are being transferred to a
> separate group in whose hands lies control." (*Ibid.*,
> pp. 67–68.)

   They did not look benignly on the corporate
managers who had succeeded to operating control
of large businesses. They referred to "a new form of

absolutism" in which "new princes" exercise power over "economic empires," relegating "owners" to the position merely of those who supply the means for the exercise of that power. (*Ibid.*, p. 124.)

Professor Berle carried these themes forward in his famous 1932 debate with another professor, Merrick Dodd. Berle believed "either you have a system based on individual ownership of property or you do not." (Berle, "For Whom Corporate Managers Are Trustees," 45 *Harvard Law Review*, 1932, p. 1368.) Since he believed "ownership" necessarily implies "control" of property and viewed the relevant property to be the enterprise itself rather than the shares of stock traded on the stock exchanges, Professor Berle could not bring himself to accept a solution that would assign to management a fiduciary duty owing to the enterprise itself. In the absence of direct managerial control by broadly dispersed shareholders, he looked, instead, to government or legal control as the only way to assure responsible conduct by corporate management.

Without it, Professor Berle thought, there would be "economic civil war" and perhaps even "successive cataclysms" that would lead to the ultimate downfall of the corporate system. (*Ibid.*, p. 1372.)

Professor Dodd, however, disclaimed the Berle notion that "managerial powers are held in trust for stockholders as sole beneficiaries of the corporate enterprise." Rather, he believed the business corporation is an "economic institution which has a social service as well as a profit-making function," and he advanced the proposition, rather novel at the time, that

"... [I]f the unity of corporate body is real, then there is reality and not simply legal fiction in the proposition that the managers of the unit are fiduciaries for it and not merely for its individual members, that they are ... trustees for an institution rather than attorneys for the stockholders." (Dodd, "For Whom Are Corporate Managers Trustees?" 45 *Harvard Law Review*, 1932, p. 1160.)

Dodd's goal was a "professional spirit of public service" on the part of business corporations. He doubted that diverse and constantly changing bodies of shareholders would fill that role. Instead, he thought that "if incorporated business is to become professionalized, it is to the managers, not to the owners, that we must look for the accomplishment of this result." (*Ibid.*, p. 1153.)

Fifty-seven years later, no one can doubt that Professor Dodd had a much clearer crystal ball than Professor Berle's. Professor Berle's "cataclysms" did not come to pass, and the age of the professional business manager with a strong sense of obligation to the amalgamated corporate enterprise, involving both stockholders and many other constituencies, including society itself, has continued to gain acceptance.

Professor Manning's 1958 Mid-Course Perception

Let me now leave 1932 and make a brief stop at a mid-course milepost, the year 1958. One of the first to perceive the futility of Berle and Means' "ownership" versus "control" concerns was Bayless Manning, a Yale University law professor and later Dean of Stanford Law School. In 1958, he directly challenged the idea that the related and then-popular notion of "corporate democracy" was competent to resolve complex corporate governance dilemmas.

Writing in the *Yale Law Journal*, he referred to the concept of corporate democracy as "a shimmering conception using good old American free enterprise with good old American Jacksonianism" and urged that "we have to proceed from the facts of the modern corporate institution and be accommodated to them, rather than to a bucolic and obsolete image." (Manning, "Book Review," 67 *Yale Law Journal*, 1958, p. 1490.) He suggested we abandon the idea that shareholders "own the corporation" and substitute the more restricted concept that the only thing they "own" is their shares of stock. In Manning's view, this conforms more closely to shareholders' own expectations and describes more accurately what they in fact handle as their own—buying, selling, and giving away. It is not even necessary, he thought, to say anything about "who owns" the corporation when discussing the problem of proper distribution of corporate power.

Professor Manning, who thought it better to deal with reality and to work out pragmatic solutions, urged

"franker acceptance that centralized managerial control is necessary, a fact and here to stay; less wishful pretense that the shareholders' vote is or can be an effective restraint; emphasis upon disclosure, free exit and transfer as the shareholder's principal protections; and development of new and extrinsic mechanics to supervise management dealings in corporate funds for nonbusiness purposes and for itself." (*Ibid.*, p. 1493.)

As we shall see, Professor Manning's 1958 analysis and his confidence in evolutionary accommodation, rather than efforts to seek compulsory restoration of a world that never was, have turned out to be largely consistent with the typically American, pragmatic, and evolutionary process that has in fact taken place and still goes on.

Development of the "Enterprise" Approach to Corporate Responsibility Before the Takeover Era

In the ensuing decades, as America unknowingly approached the takeover era of the 1980s, effective measures were taken that addressed the social and economic responsibility issues that Berle and Means thought were inherent in their intellectually insoluble separation of "ownership" from "control." These later developments reflected changing public perceptions that went both to the affirmative social obligations of American business and to the mechanism by which business enterprises should be organized. Recognition of these felt needs of society has been implemented to an extent by governmental action but, more important, by the voluntary initiative of the business community itself.

In the area of governmental action, the underlying philosophy of most federal legislation of the 1930s was "disclosure" to investors of facts material to them—not that government should tell managers how to run the business.

A different kind of governmental initiative was evidenced by legislation of the 1960s and 1970s. Government began intervening in comprehensive new ways to reflect society's view that other stakeholder constituencies in American society have legitimate interests in the way corporate enterprises are managed. Consumers and the public at large were invested with new protections by a host of new laws that greatly expanded the areas of mandated corporate responsibility, including such legislation as antidiscrimination laws, the Consumer Product Safety Act, the Environmental Quality Improvement Act, and many other environmental protection laws.

Much of this legislation, I think it fair to say, either anticipated or mirrored a rapidly progressing initiative of American business itself toward a heightened sense of social responsibility to a diversity of constituencies. Those voluntary initiatives reflected social pressures, to be sure; but they also reflected the natural acts of a changing type of person who was evolving as the manager of American business. During the 1960s and 1970s, in many corporate settings, probably a large majority of them, the senior management people were coming to be the ultimate distillation of a "meritocracy" of employees who had advanced through the system by virtue of their talents, industry, and accomplishments rather than through family connections or some other association with major shareholders or financiers—these

employees were people who were broadly representative of society at large. Supported by the country's
colleges and business schools, which taught that
managing a corporate enterprise is a professional
role to be undertaken as trustee for the shareholders
and other stakeholders, the concept of the nonown-
er "professional manager" achieved recognition.

This developing model of corporate responsibility was reflected in a variety of actions and positions
taken by business leaders during the 1970s and early 1980s. Among those was the important 1971 Statement entitled "Social Responsibilities of Business
Corporation," formulated by the Committee for
Economic Development, composed of 200 leading
businessmen and educators. That self-imposed prescription of social duty noted that "business functions by public consent, and its basic purpose is to
serve constructively the needs of society—to the satisfaction of society." However, it said:

> "The expectations of American society have now
> begun to rise at a faster pace than the nation's
> economic and social performance. . . . Fundamen-
> tal changes are also taking place in attitudes, with
> greater emphasis being put on human values—
> on individual worth and the qualitative aspects
> of life and community affairs . . . and society has
> also become acutely conscious of environmental
> problems and other social issues." (*Ibid.*, p. 12.)

Approaching an "enterprise" definition of
fiduciary responsibility, the Council called the cor-

poration a "permanent institution in society" and urged the professional manager to see the corporation as "an institution very much more enduring than himself—an institution in which he plays a significant but transient role." (*Ibid.*, p. 21.)

Facing squarely into the intellectually difficult notion of managerial responsibility to a broad array of corporate stakeholders, the Council necessarily disregarded Berle and Means' simplistic formulation, saying:

> "[T]he widely diversified nature of business ownership today alters the interest of the stockholder as classically defined. . . . Stockholders' interests, therefore, tend to ride with corporations as a group and with investment policies which provide benefits to the corporate sector as a whole—in the form of improved environmental conditions, a better labor force, and stronger public approval of private business. . . .
>
> "Inasmuch as the business community as a whole clearly has a vital stake in a good, well-functioning society, it can be argued that the stockholder's interest in the long run is best served by corporate policies which contribute to the development of the kind of society in which business can grow and prosper." (*Ibid.*, p. 30.)

Similar views were also expressed by the Business Roundtable, a group of chief executive officers of the country's largest corporations. In a 1978 statement on corporate governance ("The Role and Composition of the Board of Directors of the Large Publicly

Held Corporation," 33 *Business Lawyer*, 1978, p. 2083), they emphasized that a board's duty is to consider the overall impact of corporate activities on the society of which it is a part and that, because the interests of shareholders cannot be conceived solely in terms of short-range profit maximization, directors best serve the shareholders' interests by balancing short-range and long-term profitability.

In 1981, the Business Roundtable issued a further Statement on Corporate Responsibility that, in what has to be called a giant stride away from Berle and Means, said this:

"Balancing the shareholder's expectations of maximum return against other priorities is one of the fundamental problems confronting corporate management. The shareholder must receive a good return but the legitimate concerns of the other constituencies also must have the appropriate attention."

Corporate management, the Roundtable said, must consider in its decisionmaking all the corporation's stakeholders:

"Responsibility to all these constituents *in toto* constitutes responsibility to society, making the corporation both an economically and [a] socially viable entity. Business and society have a symbiotic relationship: the long-term viability of the corporation depends upon its responsibility to the society of which it is a part. And the well-being of society depends upon profitable and responsible business enterprises."

I have tried to outline very briefly the history and attitude and program of the corporate managerial community in America as we came into the takeover era of the 1980s—recognition of shareholders as the most important but not the exclusive constituency to which management owes a duty, emphasis on balancing the interests of diverse constituencies, and a pervasive view that the interests of society must be served in order to enable continued viability and success of private corporate enterprises.

The New Corporate Governance Model of the "Efficient Market" Theorists and Their Takeover Supporters

Now it is appropriate to consider how corporate governance has fared during the last decade. As the controversy over the reshaping of corporate America swirls around in courts and the halls of Congress, in the state legislatures and the boardrooms of America, confrontational rhetoric from both pro- and anti-takeover spokesmen would suggest little room for accommodation.

For their part, the takeover activists and arbitrageurs, and their supporters from the "efficient market" school of economics, believe the social and economic dislocation associated with some takeovers is justified by what to them is a proven and precise mechanism, whereby capital is most efficiently allo-

cated by what is called the "market for corporate control." Since Professor Henry Manne first coined that
phrase in 1965, "it has approached the status of a
truism within the 'law and economics' community
that hostile takeovers serve as the primary disci-
plinary mechanism by which corporate managements are held accountable." (Coffee, "Regulating
the Market for Corporate Control," 84 *Columbia Law
Review*, 1984, p. 1199.) Later disciples of that view say
that "the tender bidding process polices managers
. . . and disciplines or replaces them if they stray too
far from the service of the shareholders." (Frank H.
Easterbrook and Daniel F. Fischel, "The Proper Role
of a Target's Management in Responding to a Tender
Offer," 94 *Harvard Law Review*, 1981, p. 1169.)
However, others believe this ignores the impact of
other techniques, such as independent boards, shareholder voting, derivative litigation, and disclosure
statutes, that ensure managerial accountability.
(Coffee, *op. cit.*, p. 1189.)

At least during the Reagan administration, this "efficient market" view approached being official
gospel. Thus, the Council of Economic Advisers
Report that accompanied the President's annual economic report to the Congress in 1985 observed with
obvious approval that "the market for control" of
publicly held corporations determines "who will
operate the Nation's largest business enterprises"
and, relatedly, that the same market for control "in-
fluences the business strategies" many of these organizations follow. Then, in terminology reminiscent
of Berle and Means, the Council noted what was

clearly a problem in their view, namely, a separation between the "ownership" of shareholders and "control" by what are called their "hired managers."

Shareholders, they said, want share value to be maximized, whereas managers' incentives "are often more complex and can involve assurances of continued employment." Again reverting to 1932 terminology, the Council then postulated an "agency problem" by reason of this asserted divergence of incentives that, they said, can make managers "poor agents of their stockholders"; and they stated that if the problem goes "unchecked," it can "deter socially beneficial mergers, and keep assets from being allocated to higher valued uses," impede adoption of more profitable capitalization plans, and otherwise prevent publicly traded corporations from making the largest possible contributions to aggregate economic performance.

In addition, the President's advisors said, "the capital markets can be relied upon to generate a distribution of corporate governance schemes," a process they clearly looked on with favor.

This assumption that the market for corporate control is a needed constraining force on managerial business strategies, and a desirable mechanism for allocating corporate control itself, derives from a host of sophisticated writings by theorists of the so-called efficient market school. In equally voluminous criticisms, other observers suggest that the alleged discipline imposed by the market for corporate control is limited by its erratic application in a world of disparate circumstances and should really serve only as a remedy of last resort for massive managerial failures, not as the principal enforcer of corporate accountability.

These critics believe that the capability of the takeover process to identify with precision, and to replace, inefficient management is not at all clear. In fact, they suggest, just the opposite happens. One study, for example, shows that in a majority of cases the acquiring companies considered the target to be already well managed, and "their objective was not to discipline or replace poorly run companies but to own well-run ones." (John Brooks, *The Takeover Game*, Dutton, 1987, p. 227.)

Whatever one thinks of the merits of these contending propositions, however, one thing is certain: Radically new concepts of corporate governance are being advanced and implemented in our society.

What was once a rarified and academic "efficient market" theory is now being applied to actual events, and this practice continues to be rationalized by sophisticated academic authorities. As we have seen, however, they carry the baggage of Berle and Means' theoretical constructs.

For example, in a recent analysis by Professor Michael Jensen of the Harvard Business School, we are told the current restructuring of corporate America resolves a central weakness of the public corporation—what Professor Jensen calls "the conflict between owners and managers over the control and use of corporate resources." (Michael C. Jensen, Jay O. Light, and George Fisher, "Eclipse of the Public Corporation," 67 *Harvard Business Review*, Sept./Oct. 1989, p. 61.) He postulates that corporate managers often reinvest free cash flow in uneconomic projects and that it is more efficient overall to distribute that cash flow to shareholders who, he believes, will invest it more efficiently through the operation of the capital markets. Whether he is right or wrong in that is not our subject here.

What is of interest, however, is Professor Jensen's analysis that in the typical leveraged buyout, the result is what he calls "a new model of enterprise that aligns the interests of owners and managers . . . ." (*Ibid.*, p. 72.) Professor Jensen identifies this newly installed form of corporate governance under the title of "the LBO Association." That body consists of the partnership that put the arrangement together, the new managers who hold substantial equity stakes, and the institutional investors that funded the takeover. Because of the leveraging effect of the debt placed upon the corporate enterprise, the general partners and the new company managers own and control a large part of the total ownership without putting up the big investment that was formerly represented by equity of the public shareholders. This concentration of control in a few people without substantial financial investment relative to the value of the enterprise is not only justifiable, he says, but crucial to effective operation of the enterprise, because it "intensifies the ownership incentives that are so important to efficiency." (*Ibid.*, p. 69.)

He then suggests that public companies can learn from such LBO associations and should emulate many of their characteristics, including borrowing more to enable cash distributions to shareholders and increasing equity ownership of management to provide more personal incentives for efficient operations. (*Ibid.*, p. 72.)

One does not have to decide that Professor Jensen's economic analysis is wrong to observe that he has solved Berle and Means' dilemma in a way not entirely lacking in irony. His school of thought is really saying, it seems to me, that if the problem is that management "control" of a company is separated from and unresponsive to interests of the public share "owners," then the solution is for someone else to borrow money, buy out and get rid of those public "owners" of the enterprise, and replace them with people who will manage and own most of the enterprise, while making only a relatively nominal personal investment. Whether this is economically efficient in particular cases is one question. Whether in time it will prove to have been socially and economically desirable remains to be seen.

One can also ask where in this approach do we find an incentive to social responsibility by the new managers, or an incentive to serve the broad range of the company's stakeholders? As more and more publicly held enterprises "go private" and are free of the discipline of public disclosure under the securities laws, and as more and more professional managers are replaced by "LBO Association" managers whose predominant incentive is appreciation of their personal equity stake, what implications does this have for long-term economic goals of the enterprise and for society at large? One finds very little, if anything, in the vast literature of the "official market" theorists that seems to address these questions.

The Changing Nature, Motivations, and Expectations of Today's "Shareholders"

Another force that has contributed strongly to making the market for corporate control an actual determinant of corporate governance is the changing nature of America's shareholder body. Berle and Means in 1932 would have preferred to put their faith in the collective wisdom of the 5 to 8 million people who then owned stock. They would never have believed what would happen to the composition and attitude of America's body of shareholders in the present world of large institutional investors, index options and futures contracts, market index funds, index arbitrage, and computerized program trading. Their individual investor who buys stock in a particular company as a long-term "investment" is, as I am sure you know, a vanishing breed in America.

We have it on good authority that the public and private employee pension funds of America hold over 24 percent of the total market value of all outstanding equities in publicly traded corporations. (Harvey H. Segal, *Corporate Makeover*, Viking, 1989, p. 81.) Combined with all other pools of institutional investor money, the percentage is closer to 50. Those moneys are invested by the fund managers on behalf of many millions of individual investors, as well as of working and retired employees of corporations and governmental units around the country.

This institutional power may be even more concentrated in a few investment managers than the foregoing statistics would suggest. According to a recent study of 511 large corporations, "On average, the five largest stockholders in these 511 corporations control about 25 percent of the corporation's shares, and the 20 largest stockholders control about 38 percent of the corporation's shares." (Ira Millstein, Statement to House Committee on Education and Labor, February 8, 1989.)

We have come a long way, it seems, from the broadly dispersed individual shareholder power indicated by the "People's Capitalism" promoted in the 1950s by the New York Stock Exchange and may be returning, in a very different form, to a concentration of economic power that could be reminiscent of one of the problems that so troubled Berle and Means in 1932.

Portfolio turnover for pension funds is very high, so their participants are merely temporary shareholders in many cases. It is also clear that many pension-fund managers have been "active takeover players" in the market for corporate control. One of the reasons these managers are motivated to take short-term profits by tendering stock into tender offers, and to vote against antitakeover defense mechanisms presented at shareholder meetings, is what they perceive to be the constraints of a fiduciary or statutory duty, owed to the pension fund beneficiaries, always to maximize current investment results and take advantage of immediate profit-making opportunities.

Also, in the name of "investment" performance, many pension fund managers actively look for stocks that might be takeover targets in the near term.

(See Martin Lipton, "Corporate Governance in the Age of Finance Corporatism," 136 *University of Pennsylvania Law Review*, 1987, p. 7.) This desire for quick profit has contributed to highly leveraged takeovers because institutional investors and takeover arbitrageurs, once they believe a target company is "in play," buy in hopes of a quick resale at a profit to either the acquirer of the company or another market participant.

Many observers believe this short-term profit mentality, evident in segments of the institutional investor community, is having an undesirable impact on corporate strategies by influencing managers to adopt short-term financial engineering measures to enhance stock value at the expense of important long-term development programs. A former Commissioner of the Securities and Exchange Commission puts it this way:

"Inevitably the short-term perspective of institutional investors breeds similar perspectives in management. Realizing the tentativeness of the ownership of large amounts of their company's stock, and sensitive to the market penalties accruing to short-term adverse performance, management perspective is necessarily foreshortened and the maintenance of quarter-to-quarter earnings improvement becomes a paramount goal. . . ." (A. A. Sommer, Jr., Introduction to James F. Hogg, *The Predator and the Predatee*, National Legal Center for the Public Interest, 1988, p. viii.)

Ira Millstein, Chairman of a Pension Fund Task Force appointed by the Governor of New York, presents a similar analysis. Suggesting state and federal legislative changes to encourage long-term investment policies by pension funds and to confirm that it is legally permissible for fund fiduciaries to forgo immediate short-term gains in response to tender offers, Mr. Millstein has noted:

> "It is corporate managers' perception that to raise stock prices and keep entrepreneurial bidders away, companies must utilize short-term solutions at the expense of the long-term research and development, training of employees and reinvestment in new and existing plants necessary for future growth and competitiveness. Whether this perception is in fact correct is not terribly important; this perception seems to be driving much short-term corporate decision-making. The point for us is that pension funds seem all too willing to further this perception by quickly, and perhaps automatically, accepting immediate benefits and riskier higher yields to fuel those immediate benefits."

These trends pose important new questions relating to corporate governance—questions that go to institutional shareholder responsibility to the enterprise and its various stakeholders.

As Mr. Millstein and many others are suggesting, it seems clear that ways should be found to redesign pension fund investment incentives on a socially responsible basis so that their trustees and managers are motivated to support long-term investment in the companies where they place money on behalf of their millions of beneficiaries and to support the programs of corporate managers who seek to invest and reinvest capital for the long term.

The "Enterprise" Theory of Corporate Responsibility

To recapitulate briefly, we have the "efficient market" theorists' view that corporate business plans should be responsive to the market for corporate control and that many of the "governance" decisions concerning *who* should manage large business enterprises should themselves be a function of that same mechanism. In fact, those theories are being transformed into reality, in large part because of the short-term profit mentality of many institutional investors, to say nothing of the takeover arbitrage speculators.

Where does this leave corporate directors and the professional manager whose training, experience, and instincts are identified with long-term investment strategies, continued viability of the enterprise, responsibility for stable and growing shareholder return over time, and service to the entire array of the corporation's stakeholders?

Resolution of many of these issues, fortunately, is being addressed in what appears to be an increasingly constructive way by the courts of America and, most important, by the courts of the state of Delaware. The decisions of the Delaware courts govern many of these events because a large majority of companies is incorporated there.

In the many takeover-related cases decided during the 1980s, it is true, the Delaware judges have been careful to respect the classical definitions pertaining to directors' fiduciary duty to shareholders. At the same time, it seems to me the judges have appreciated the need to adjust the governing rules, on an evolutionary basis, so as to recognize society's needs and expectations in relation to the turbulent takeover cases that come before them.

One of the major control issues, if one can put it in a single, oversimplified sentence, has been the conflict betweeen shareholder opportunity to realize short-term takeover profits, on the one hand, and, on the other, management desire to preserve the enterprise and continue implementation of long-term business plans.

The intellectual dilemma the courts have to face in these situations derives from the prescription in the corporation laws of most states, including Delaware, that responsibility is assigned to boards of directors to "manage the business and affairs of the corporation." Does that embrace decisions that have the effect and intent of prohibiting shareholders who may want to sell their shares from doing so or of discouraging tender offers that could produce short-term profits for the shareholders? On the face of it, one might not think so. Yet the developing case law does in certain settings permit the directors in effect to control whether shareholders can sell, or be provided an opportunity to sell, their shares. How can this be?

In a series of decisions, the Delaware courts have evolved a set of formulations that one can characterize as resting on an underlying premise that, while maximizing shareholder value is important, the directors' primary duty—their assigned area of fiduciary responsibility—is to the corporate "enterprise," broadly defined.

Let me be more precise. Under the time-honored concept of the "business judgment rule," the courts in Delaware as elsewhere presume that the directors of a corporation, in making a corporate business decision, acted on an informed basis, in good faith, and in the honest belief that the action taken was in the best interests of the company. Of course, this does not apply if the directors are not disinterested, that is, have some conflict between their self-interest and the interest of the corporation. The Delaware cases on takeovers, simply put, address the validity of takeover defense measures adopted by corporate directors by testing whether their action satisfies the standards of the business judgment rule just mentioned.

In the recent cases, the Delaware courts have upheld a variety of antitakeover measures where they were approved in the exercise of business judgment by a majority board of nonmanagement outside directors considered to be free of potentially conflicting interests. What is new here is that among the important considerations entitled to recognition under these cases is a board's decision that the takeover might pose a danger to "corporate policy" or to the "corporate enterprise" itself. There is a difference between that objective and the traditional focus only on shareholder interests.

However, it was not until the 1989 Time-Warner decision that it became clear the courts will support a judgment by corporate directors that their fundamental duty is continued dedication to corporate "enterprise" goals in the long-term interest of the enterprise and of whatever investors might comprise its body of shareholders over time, even when that judgment is directly counter to the wishes of the company's current (and, one might say, increasingly transitory) shareholders.

As many of you know, Time Incorporated (the company that publishes *Time* magazine) had agreed to merge with Warner Communications under arrangements that would have involved putting that merger to a vote of the Time shareholders. The date for the shareholder meeting had actually been set when Paramount announced an offer to purchase from the Time shareholders all their stock at $175 per share. Just a few months earlier, the stock had been trading at slightly more than $100, and it is clear that most institutional and other shareholders wanted to sell at the tender offer price. Time and Warner did not want that to happen, so they revised the arrangement in such a way that a shareholder vote was not involved. By doing so, they avoided a negative vote by the shareholders who would have liked to defeat the merger and sell to Paramount, which had by then increased its offer to $200.

The court upheld the position of the Time directors, so the shareholders never had an opportunity to accept Paramount's tender offer. The basis for the court's decision is very interesting.

The Time directors had explained to the court that they had a long-term business plan for their company that could be possible only by way of defeating Paramount's tender offer and completing the arrangements with Warner; also, they said that the board considered it important to maintain an independent Time Inc. that reflected a distinctive Time "corporate culture" and that they believed the long-term value to shareholders from the Time-Warner combination would ultimately be superior to the tender offer price being offered by Paramount. Without deciding whether that long-term value would or would not in fact come to pass, the court concluded that

"Delaware law does recognize that directors, when acting deliberately, in an informed way, and in the good faith pursuit of corporate interests, may follow a course designed to achieve long-term value even at the cost of immediate value maximization." (*Paramount v. Time*, Chancery Ct. #10866, pp. 50–51.)

The court then addressed the shareholders' argument that goes to the heart of the corporate governance "control" issue, namely, whether the directors' duty of loyalty to shareholders required them "to afford to the shareholders the power and opportunity to designate whether the company should now be sold." Persuaded that the transaction being pursued by the Time board had its origins and central purpose in good-faith strategic business planning for the corporate enterprise, the court reached the following conclusion:

> "The value of a shareholder's investment, over time, rises or falls chiefly because of the skill, judgment and perhaps luck—for it is present in all human affairs—of the managers and directors of the enterprise. When they exercise sound or brilliant judgment, shareholders are likely to profit; when they fail to do so, share values will likely fail to appreciate. In either event, the financial vitality of the corporation and the value of a company's shares is in the hands of the directors and managers of the firm. The corporation law does not operate on the theory that directors, in exercising their powers to manage the firm, are obligated to follow the wishes of a majority of shareholders. In fact, directors, not shareholders, are charged with the duty to manage the firm. . . .
>
> "In the decision they have reached here, the Time Board may be proven in time to have been brilliantly right or dismayingly wrong. In this decision, as in other decisions affecting the financial value of their investment, the shareholders will bear the effects for good or ill. That many, presumably most, shareholders would prefer the Board to do otherwise than it has done does not, in the circumstances of a challenge to this type of a transaction[,] . . . afford a basis to interfere with the Board's business judgment." (*Ibid.*, pp. 77–78.)

To students of the evolving Delaware court decisions, the holding in the Time-Warner case, while very significant, was not entirely surprising as a logical evolution from other Delaware decisions over the past few years. For more distant observers of the corporate governance subject, especially those still enamored of the Berle and Means ownership and control formulation of 1932, that decision may seem rather more dramatic. It was, to be sure, carefully constructed to focus only on the precise situation at hand. Nonetheless, it deals squarely with the question whether there are occasions when directors should effectively subordinate the short-term wishes of current shareholders and give priority instead to the long-term interests of the business enterprise and its shareholders as a continuing body. The court's clear answer was that they can, and they should.

To conclude, then, I suggest history and logic have both shown that in the publicly held corporation a constructive corporate governance analysis cannot be based on simplistic notions of who does or does not own the assets and business of the corporation.

Nor does worrying about relating ownership to "control" get us much further. The control mechanism of publicly held American corporations is, to be sure, structurally imprecise and multifaceted, but it does exist and it has been generally effective. The fact is that boards and managers are subject to a broad and complex body of effective "controls"— the "control" of operating in the fishbowl mandated by disclosure requirements of the securities laws, the "control" of a host of substantive laws and regulations that society has imposed to govern broad segments of corporate activity, the significant role of outside directors who are increasingly commissioned by the courts to govern takeover-related and similar corporate decisions under strict and precise rules, the "control" of shareholder election of directors, the "control" of shareholder expectations regarding value of their investment, the "control" of meeting society's expectations in order to support long-term viability of the enterprise, and, not unimportant, the "control" inherent in most professional managers' personal instinct and desire to perform well, efficiently, and honorably and to be perceived as doing so.

One could hope that an emerging consensus in our society—a consensus that looks to the "enterprise" nature of corporate business and corporate responsibility—together with institutional responses such as the Delaware court's recent pronouncement in the Time-Warner case, will continue to inspire respect for efforts of corporate boards and managements to implement well-considered and socially responsible business strategies to the benefit first and foremost of long-term shareholder value but also in the interest of society and all its stakeholders.

If this occurs, and if the institutional investor community can reorient its investment policies to long-term goals, moderating its contribution to the speculative atmosphere and abusive practices evident in the market for corporate control, then we could expect that the country's many well-managed business enterprises will continue without undue distraction in their fruitful mission, which has produced in America a level of material well-being and social stability unparalleled elsewhere in the world.

LABOR AND THE ECONOMY: TOWARD A "KINDER AND GENTLER" SOCIETY

by

Benjamin Aaron

Benjamin Aaron

Benjamin Aaron is Professor of Law, Emeritus, at the University of California, Los Angeles. Professor Aaron received an A.B. degree from the University of Michigan in 1937 and an LL.B. degree from Harvard Law School in 1940. He was admitted to the Illinois bar in 1941. He joined the staff of the UCLA Institute of Industrial Relations in 1946, following four years of service as a staff member and Executive Director of the National War Labor Board in Washington, D.C., and a brief tour of duty as a member of a labor advisory commission to the Supreme Commander, Allied Powers, in Tokyo, Japan.

Professor Aaron served as a research associate and later as Associate Director of the Institute, and in 1960, he became Director, a position he held for 15 years. Also in 1960, he joined the faculty of the UCLA School of Law as Professor of Law. He became Emeritus Professor of Law as of July 1, 1986.

In 1951–52, Professor Aaron served by presidential appointment as a public member and later Vice Chairman of the National Wage Stabilization Board. In 1968 he served as Chairman of the Consultants' Committee that drafted the Los Angeles County Employee Relations Ordinance. In 1972–73 he served as Chairman of the California Assembly's Advisory Council on Public Employee Relations. Since 1946 he has arbitrated labor disputes in virtually every major industry. In 1981 he was the recipient of the American Arbitration Association's Distinguished Service Award.

Professor Aaron has twice been appointed to the faculty of the Salzburg Seminar (1958, 1967) and has been a Resident Fellow at the Center for Advanced Study in the Behavioral Sciences (1966–67); a Visiting Fellow at Clare Hall, University of Cambridge, England (1973), and at Australian National University (1981); and Phi Beta Kappa Visiting Scholar (1978–79). He is a past President of the National Academy of Arbitrators (1962), the Industrial Relations Research Association (1972), and the International Society for Labor Law and Social Security (1985–88).

Professor Aaron is the author and editor of numerous articles and books on labor law and industrial relations.

LABOR AND THE ECONOMY: TOWARD A "KINDER AND GENTLER" SOCIETY
by
Benjamin Aaron

In his inaugural address President Bush declared that "America is never wholly herself unless she is engaged in high moral principle." He stated that our national purpose is "to make kinder the face of the nation and gentler the face of the world." (*Vital Speeches of the Day*, Vol. 55, No. 9, Feb. 15, 1989, p. 259.) In this paper I propose to focus on a few areas in which new legislation and business and administrative policies affecting labor are needed to transform the President's lofty purposes into reality. My discussion will concentrate on five broad areas: education and training, worker remuneration, security of employment, conditions of employment, and the administration of laws affecting discrimination in employment.

Education and Training

The problem of unemployment in this country is becoming, increasingly, a structural one; that is to say, the skill levels required for newly created jobs are higher than the skills possessed by many job seekers. Indeed, an increasing proportion of new entrants into the work force lacks the basic qualifications to hold even relatively unskilled jobs. As the Ford Foundation Project on Social Welfare and the American

Future has recently pointed out:

"Too many young Americans are failing to make an adequate transition from school to work. They drift aimlessly through their young adulthood— often with disastrous consequences. There has been a growing inequality between the prospects of those who attend college and those who do not. The latter are finding it increasingly difficult to obtain a decent job, start a career, and support a family." (*The Common Good: Social Welfare and the American Future*, Ford Foundation, 1989, p. 30.)

The statistics are appalling. Approximately one in four American teenagers leaves high school before receiving a diploma. About 40 percent of Hispanic students leave before finishing high school, and among blacks in some urban areas the dropout rate is almost 50 percent. High school dropouts are two and one-half times more likely than graduates to be without a job, three and one-half times more likely to be arrested for a crime, and seven and one-half times more likely to be dependent on public assistance. The proportion of 18- to 24-year-olds not employed, not enrolled in school, and not in the military has almost doubled during the past 20 years to approximately 12 percent for white males and more than doubled to almost 30 percent for nonwhite males. (*Ibid.*)

In recent testimony before a Department of Labor Commission on Workforce Quality and Labor Market Efficiency, William Wiggenhorn, Corporate Vice

President and Director of Training and Education of Motorola, Inc., pointed out that 75 percent of the American work force in the year 2000 is in the work force today and that 20 to 30 million of these workers have serious problems with basic skills. Specifically, he said that they "cannot read, write, speak English, calculate, solve problems, or communicate well enough to function effectively on the job or in their everyday lives." Wiggenhorn added that half of Motorola's 24,000 U. S. production workers possess basic skills below seventh-grade level. (Bureau of National Affairs, Inc. (BNA), *Daily Labor Report,* No. 82, May 10, 1989, pp. A-2 –A-3.)

The fact is that, especially in our big cities, we are in danger of losing generations of young people who drop out of school, become unemployable, and sink into a permanent underclass characterized by poverty, with all its attendant ills, and a high crime rate. Greatly improved education is a necessary, if not a sufficient, requirement if this trend is to be reversed. Over 20 years ago, the National Commission on Technology, Automation, and Economic Progress appointed by President Johnson said in its Report:

"From the purely economic point of view, education has three principal effects: (1) It can increase the versatility and adaptability of people with respect to vocations and thus increase their capacity to adjust to change; (2) it can open up increasing opportunity to persons who otherwise might have difficulty in finding and holding employment; and (3) it can increase the productivi-

ty of workers at any level of skill or ability.
Though education is much more than a means
of economic progress, it is a decisive factor in the
economic advancement of any country." (*Technology and the American Economy*, Vol. 1, 1966, p. 44.)

Of course, improved formal education cannot, in
itself, provide a complete solution to the problem.
As the Ford Foundation report recognized,

"growing numbers of young Americans are
trapped by a complex of interconnected problems: leaving school early, teen parenthood, welfare dependency, joblessness, delinquency, and an
unstable family life. Too often in the past, attention and resources have shifted from one thread
to another, with efforts directed at dealing with
the concern of the moment. . . . These efforts have
led to a growing recognition that those in greatest
need are suffering from not just one problem but
many, and that greater effort, more resources, and
more time will be needed to help them." (*Op. cit.*,
p. 34.)

What is required is a diversified approach that ad-
dresses a number of objectives. School dropout rates
can be reduced by concerted action aimed at expanding the life options of disadvantaged young people,
by offering personal incentives to remain in school,
and by improving schools by providing for decentralized decisionmaking so that it takes place at the
level of the individual school, thus allowing prin-

cipals and teachers more autonomy and independence and giving teachers greater freedom to develop innovative programs for students in and outside the classroom. Collaboration between schools and businesses can also be helpful, especially in serving the needs of the most at-risk, disadvantaged youths. There is evidence that serious school-business partnerships have achieved some success in their efforts to increase school attendance, reduce dropout rates, and improve academic performance. Experiments combining remedial education with part-time work and other services have produced encouraging results, as have summer programs combining work, education, and counseling. (*Ibid.*, pp. 35–42.)

A closely related problem that also must be addressed is that of teen pregnancy. More than one million teenage girls become pregnant each year in this country, and nearly 470,000 give birth. Girls under age 15 are five times more likely to give birth than young adolescents in any other developed country for which data are available. Early childbearers are much more likely than those who have their children later to experience economic hardships and family disruption in later life, to drop out of school, and to fail to find stable and remunerative employment. The proportion of teenage mothers becoming welfare recipients under the Aid to Families with Dependent Children (AFDC) program is increasing. Moreover, they and their children make up the bulk of those who remain on the welfare rolls for extended periods. (*Ibid.*, p. 43.) The proportion of teenage mothers who are unmarried and are addicted to drugs is high. In the absence of successful efforts to wean them away from drugs and to get them back into school, both they and their children will be condemned to a life of poverty and despair.

All students of the education and training problem agree that present methods of on-the-job training are inadequate. A Massachusetts Institute of Technology (MIT) commission recently called for a new blending of technology and human resources that would treat the U. S. work force "as an asset rather than a cost." It warned that "without major changes in the ways schools and firms train workers over the course of a lifetime, no amount of macroeconomic fine-tuning and technological innovation will be able to produce significantly improved economic performance and a rising standard of living." The commission faulted U. S. training techniques as consisting of little more than telling a new worker to "follow Joe around" to learn the ropes and noted that companies in other countries are more likely to be seen as "learning institutions" that prepare workers with broad, flexible skills to be used over the longer term. The commission also deplored that Americans "systematically undervalue the worth of having employees who are well-educated and whose skills are continuously developed." As demographic trends bring increasing numbers of new entrants into the work force from historically disadvantaged groups, it warned, "these self-imposed handicaps are likely to have more serious consequences." The commission called for the cultivation of a "new economic citizenship" in which the work force is involved, educated, and rewarded. New technologies, it said, offer "an unprecedented opportunity for workers at all levels to master their work environment and increase their job satisfaction." (BNA, *Daily Labor Report*, No. 84, May 3, 1989, pp. A-14, A-15.)

Criticism of training programs comes from a variety of sources. A new report by the American Society for Training and Development (financed by the Department of Labor) declares that government policies aimed at encouraging increases and improvements in employer-based training "are conspicuously absent in the nation's investment portfolio." The report denounces the lack of an on-the-job "learning infrastructure," which it terms the "missing link in the partnership between schools and employers." The report's authors point out not only that there is a scarcity of job-related training but that those programs that do exist are unevenly distributed among the population, with an emphasis on white-collar and highly technical employees. They maintain that the "ideal device for expanding employer-based training would be some form of investment incentive for new training," preferably delivered through the tax code. (Anthony P. Carnevale and Leila J. Gainer, *The Learning Enterprise*, U. S. Department of Labor, 1989, *passim.*)

In addition, the authors point out that technological and economic change not only have increased entry-level skill requirements and the need for skill upgrading while on the job but have also "reduced the commitment between employer and employees, forcing the latter to take responsibility for their own employment security and career development." To help workers shoulder these new responsibilities, the

authors call for an increased commitment on the part
of government, which will have to assist both employers and workers in paying for such necessary services
as job retraining, portable pensions and health care
coverage, day care, and parental leave. Employers,
too, must share the responsibility for new programs.
The authors recommend that employers communicate to schools new knowledge and changing skill requirements, give more weight to educational
attainment and achievement when hiring, and work
with educators to provide "learning and earning"
curriculums that combine academic and applied
learning experiences. (*Ibid.*)

Authors Sar Levitan and Frank Gallo of the George
Washington University Center for Social Policy
Studies have recently issued a report on training and
employing the disadvantaged. They contend that
"federal neglect" has undermined job training programs designed to enhance the skills of the poor and
the unemployed. They point out that employment
and training programs have received more recent
funding cuts than have any other social programs,
with 1989 appropriations equal to only 30 percent
of the 1981 level after adjustments for inflation have
been taken into account. The authors call upon the
Department of Labor to ensure that those most in
need of assistance are served by requiring local program administrators to test applicants' reading and
mathematics skills and to consider their income, employment history, and educational attainment during the screening process. The authors also suggest
that the Department establish uniform standards for

the content of competency-based programs and con-duct spot-check audits of contractors that provide job training services to ensure the integrity of the per-formance standards system. (BNA, *Daily Labor Report,* No. 88, May 9, 1989, p. A-6.)

Levitan and Gallo have several suggestions for con-gressional action. They recommend both liberaliz-ing current limits on support service expenditures to allow for the broader use of stipends scaled to the income and financial resources of participants in job training programs and requiring that one-fourth of funds allocated to the summer youth employment program be spent on basic education. With respect to the current targeted jobs tax credit program, the authors note that the credit "unduly rewards indus-tries with large numbers of low-wage, high-turnover occupations." They suggest that credit be restruc-tured to encourage employers to hire individuals for better-paying jobs and to retain them for longer peri-ods. They also oppose subsidies to employers for workers who have already been hired.

All these problems require an increased commit-ment of funds and human resources at the federal, state, and local levels. Federal programs now avail-able include the Job Training Partnership Act (JTPA), the Job Corps, summer job programs, Chap-ter 1 of the 1981 Education Consolidation and Im-provement Act, and the Magnet Schools Assistance Program. The federal government cannot do the job alone, however; it needs massive assistance from state, local, and privately funded programs, and all of those need to be coordinated in order to achieve the maximum effect.

Worker Remuneration

A. Minimum Wage

The present statutory minimum wage in this country is a disgrace. It was last adjusted by Congress in 1977, with the current $3.35 per hour rate taking effect on January 1, 1981. In the ensuing eight years, the purchasing power of the minimum wage declined almost 38.5 percent; the $3.35 per hour in effect in 1981 is worth only $2.46 per hour in 1989 dollars. The 1989 minimum wage represents only 35 percent of average hourly earnings, a decline from 46.2 percent in 1981 and from 55.4 percent in 1968. The original minimum wage of 25 cents per hour adopted in 1938 represented a greater percentage of average hourly earnings than does $3.35 per hour in 1989. (Report of the Senate Committee on Labor and Human Resources on Minimum Wage Restoration Act of 1989, 101st Cong., 1st Sess., 1989, S. 4, p. 14.)

In two-thirds of the states, basic welfare benefits provide greater cash income than does full-time work at the current minimum wage. Thus, many of the poor cannot afford to work at the current minimum wage because it is easier for these families to survive by not working. (*Ibid.*)

Data provided by the U. S. Department of Labor in 1989 show that there were over 14 million hourly workers earning less than $4.65 per hour. Women, who make up about 45 percent of the labor force, represented over 63 percent of those who earned less than that amount. Blacks and Hispanics also represented significantly higher percentages of those low-wage workers than they did of the work force in general. Contrary to the common assumption that most low-wage earners were teenagers, this group accounted for only 27 percent of the total. Of hourly workers 65 years of age and older, 38 percent earned less than $4.65 per hour. (*Ibid.*)

Over 6.5 million of these low-wage earners were full-time workers. Over 3.8 million were heads of households, and over 2.1 million of these worked full-time. There were 2.4 million hourly workers making less than $4.65 per hour who were officially characterized as "poor"; of these, 1.2 million were heads of households, supporting 2.1 million family members. (*Ibid.*)

To help remedy this situation, Congress in 1989 adopted amendments to the Fair Labor Standards Act (FLSA) that would, among other things, have raised the current minimum wage of $3.35 per hour to $3.85 in 1989 and to $4.25 and $4.55, respectively, in the next two years. The types and number of small businesses that would have been exempted from paying the minimum wage would have been increased, with the small-business exemption being raised to $500,000 from the current threshold of $362,500.

President Bush vetoed this bill, and Congress could not muster sufficient votes to override the veto. I think the President's action was a serious mistake, grounded on the false assumptions that the increased minimum wage would result in the loss of as many as 650,000 job opportunities and would have a significant adverse effect on the employment of teenagers and young adults. Congress had the advantage, however, of more recent data than those relied upon by the administration for its estimates. These data resulted in an estimate by qualified economists that the teenage job loss associated with a 10 percent increase in the minimum wage would equal only six-tenths of one percent and would have no significant effect on the employment of young adults aged 20 to 24. (*Ibid.*, p. 32.)

Another estimate put the job loss resulting from the increased minimum wage at only about 90,000, but even that figure is too high, primarily because it did not take into consideration that twelve states and the District of Columbia have already increased their minimum wages above the federal level. The inflationary impact of the proposed higher minimum wage is assumed by government experts to be between two- and three-tenths of a percentage point per year—equivalent to the systemwide effects of a ten-cent increase in the price of gasoline. In its report, however, the Senate Committee on Labor and Human Resources argued that these estimates are also too high. It pointed out, for example, that because the gap between the current minimum and the average wage is much greater than it was when these estimates were made, the impact today would be less. The Committee contends that a lower minimum wage, in relation to other wages in the economy, means a lesser inflationary "ripple effect" on these other wages as some are adjusted to maintain wage differentials. (*Ibid.*, pp. 26–27.)

There is considerable debate whether the proposed new minimum wage would actually help the working poor. In a letter to the *New York Times*, Professor David Ellwood of Harvard's Kennedy School and Robert Greenstein and Isaac Shapiro, Director and Senior Research Analyst, respectively, of the Center on Budget and Policy Priorities, asserted that the minimum wage is important to many of the more than 5 million poor people who live in households with a full-time, year-around worker. They pointed out that in 1987 nearly three of every five poor workers paid at an hourly rate earned $4.35 or less. Thus, a large percentage of the working poor would be affected by the proposed increase in the minimum wage. Today, they stated, full-time work at the minimum wage leaves a family of three $2,900 below the poverty line, and the same family would need a minimum wage of $5.40 per hour in 1992 to return to the poverty line. Indeed, an increase in the minimum wage to $4.45 per hour in 1992 would only partly restore the ground lost in the eight years since the minimum wage was last changed, in 1981. In fact, such a wage increase would yield a minimum wage that would be below the level of any year from 1956 to 1986, after adjusting for inflation. The writers of the letter proposed a simple goal: "[I]f the family has a full-time year-around worker, the family and its children should not have to live in poverty." They concluded that although an increased minimum wage would not, in itself, achieve that goal and that other measures, such as an expanded earned income tax credit, are also desirable, an increased minimum wage would be an important step in the right direction. (*New York Times*, Letters, April 10, 1989, p. A14, col. 4.)

Historically, each proposed increase in the minimum wage since the Fair Labor Standards Act was enacted in 1938 has been preceded by dire predictions by some economists and elements in the business community that the increase would have deleterious effects on inflation and employment. On each such occasion these predictions have not been borne out by succeeding events. The benefits of the increase in purchasing power of poor workers have outweighed any losses of employment opportunities, and the increased minimum wage has had a negligible effect on inflation. The most frequent argument heard today against increasing the minimum wage is that employers will refuse to hire, or to continue to employ, young and inexperienced workers, who, it is alleged, are simply not worth the higher minimum wage. Such claims are greatly exaggerated. Most jobs offered at the minimum wage are relatively unskilled. The Fair Labor Standards Amendments Act of 1989 passed by Congress would have increased the earnings and reduced the poverty of millions of American workers, with little or no discernible adverse impact on the economy. In vetoing it, President Bush did a great disservice to the nation.

(Shortly after this was written, Congress and the President agreed on a compromise bill that will increase the minimum wage to $3.80 per hour in 1990 and $4.25 in 1991. The bill also provides for a so-called training wage for teenagers of $3.35 per hour in the first year and $3.61 in the second. The training wage can be paid to a particular worker for no more than six months. This niggardly package is better than nothing, but it is less than the situation demands.)

B. Income and Inequality

Beginning in the 1970s, and especially during the 1980s, government, business, and industry emphasized the need to make the goods we produce more competitive in the world economy. This objective has forced American workers to compete with workers in Third World countries, whose wages and working conditions are substantially below what has been achieved in this country. Especially during the past two decades, in the name of competition and efficiency, wages were reduced in a number of key industries in the United States, and many workers who had worked for years with one employer or in a single industry were permanently laid off. In some industries, so-called two-tier wage systems were introduced; under these systems new hires were paid substantially less than those already employed and often did not attain the higher level for a number of years. Moreover, the recession of the early 1980s led many employers to push, successfully, for a general reduction in wages and fringe benefits and a relaxation or elimination of existing work rules. These changes affected organized and unorganized workers alike.

As usual, these changes have had the greatest impact on the poorest element in our society. In addition, they have contributed to the growing disparity of income between the rich and the poor. Between

1979 and 1987, the average household income of the poorest one-fifth of Americans fell from $5,439 to $5,107 (6.1 percent) in 1987 dollars, while that of the richest one-fifth rose from $61,917 to $68,775 (11.1 percent). If the years 1973 to 1978 are added in, the trend becomes clearer—an 11.8 percent loss for the poorest fifth and a 24.1 percent gain for the richest. These figures are cited to support the claims of some that the middle class has stopped growing and that the United States is on its way to becoming a two-class society. (James Lardner, "Rich, Richer; Poor, Poorer," *New York Times*, April 19, 1989, p. A19, col. 1, citing a study released by the House Ways and Means Committee in March 1989.)

Three Brookings Institution scholars, Robert E. Litan, Robert Z. Lawrence, and Charles L. Schultze, wrote recently that although compensation per worker and median family incomes both grew roughly 3 percent a year between 1950 and 1973, they have hardly moved since. They reject as an explanation that this stagnation has been caused by a falling share of "good jobs" in the economy and by the employment of a rising proportion of the work force in service industries, where wages are lower than in traditional manufacturing jobs. Rather, they argue that the dominant causes of slow income growth have been macroeconomic in nature—a productivity slowdown and the two oil shocks. These scholars, while conceding that the middle class—families earning between $20,000 and $50,000 (in 1987 dollars)—has definitely shrunk, point out that most families moving out of it have moved up. At the same time, they note that just the reverse has happened among poorer American families. Although the percentage of families earning less than $20,000 has not gone up, the proportion in it with incomes below $10,000 has. In 1973, 10 percent of America's children lived in the poorest families; by 1986 that number had risen to 16 percent. At least one-third of the nation's children now live in families with annual incomes below $20,000. By contrast, the proportion of children in families with annual incomes above $50,000 has risen, reflecting more two-earner families. This rising inequality among children has created an inequality of prospects that poses a serious challenge to the nation. (Robert E. Litan, Robert Z. Lawrence, and Charles L. Schultze, "Improving American Living Standards," *The Brookings Review*, Winter 1988/89, pp. 25–26.)

The way to combat these trends is not to reduce wages still further but to increase productivity and improve managerial efficiency. The Brookings scholars indicate a number of changes in government policy that could increase productivity. These include "increasing government funding for technological research; shifting the emphasis in 'R & D' toward development; and retaining the tax credit for private research and development expenditures." (*Ibid*, p. 30.) Basically, however, they assert that the lion's share of the responsibility for improving productivity rests with American business. They state:

"American managers must learn from their foreign competitors, adopting and improving upon technology developed in other countries. Ameri-

can companies could reap greater benefits by paying closer attention to incremental improvements
in technology as their Japanese counterparts do,
rather than betting scarce R & D funds heavily on
finding dramatic breakthroughs." (*Ibid.*)

The MIT commission report previously referred
to cited the failure in labor-management cooperation
as a significant contributor to weakness in productivity. It argued that sustained cooperation has been
limited by "deep-seated anti-union attitudes among
managers and a corresponding distrust by union
leaders of new forms of employee participation and
work organization." The commission recommended,
among other things, that organizational hierarchies
should be restructured into new job categories to promote cooperation and that partnerships should be
established between business, labor, government,
universities, and localities "as a way of overcoming
the defects of the market, which undersupplies certain collective factors that are essential to economic
success." (*Op. cit.*, pp. A-15–A-16.)

However productivity is increased, we must not
forget the needs of our poorest workers. America has
always regarded itself as a land of opportunity; we
should not permit it to become a country in which
the lowest-paid workers are deprived of all hope of
improving their lot. Recent evidence gained in a
study of the underclass conducted by the Louis Harris organization for the NAACP Legal Defense and
Educational Fund tends to refute two ideas that have
attained wide currency: One is that the poor com-

prising the underclass have lost hope of extricating themselves; the second is that middle-income people worry only about their own careers and feel no obligation to care for the less fortunate. For the study, the Harris organization interviewed a cross section of black members of the underclass in Atlanta, Chicago, Detroit, Houston, Los Angeles, New York, Philadelphia, and St. Louis. The only areas sampled were those where 40 percent or more of the population lives in poverty. When asked to name the most important changes that might improve their lives, those interviewed offered these top three responses: "better job opportunities," "more schooling available," and "more job training." More direct help from government, including handouts, was far down the list. When asked what they wanted most for their children, they said their top four aspirations were "learning to stay in school" (59 percent); "getting proper training to hold down good jobs" (58 percent); "earning enough money to be able to afford decent housing" (36 percent); and "being respected by other people" (28 percent). (Louis Harris, "Examine These Myths of the 80's," *New York Times*, May 19, 1989, p. A15, col. 2.)

With respect to the other popular notion refuted by his study, Harris reported that more than 9 in 10 Americans would support special school programs for underclass children beginning at age eight, and favor starting a Youth Corps program, with camps where both black and white young people would be taught how to read, write, organize themselves, and function productively. A like number support giving business incentives to locate workplaces in areas where the underclass lives. More than 8 in 10 Americans are in favor of "requiring the underclass people to have a job or be in a job-training program to qualify for welfare payments," but they also favor giving certain benefits, including their transportation, child care, and health care costs, to those working. (*Ibid.*)

As Harris points out, there is a "great irony" in his findings: "The expressed needs of the black underclass turn out to be precisely what society is willing to provide: education, job training, child care, etc." (*Ibid.*) The nation's task is gradually to translate that consensus into reality.

Security of Employment

A. Plant Closures, Removals, and Mass Permanent Layoffs

The United States lags behind the other industrialized democracies in protecting workers from the effects of sudden job loss caused by plant closures or removals without prior notice. (Aaron, "Plant Closings: American and Comparative Perspectives," 59 *Chicago Kent Law Review*, 1984, pp. 941–967.) American industry has been implacable in its opposition to legislation that would place any limitation on the freedom of the individual employer to shut down or move its plant for economic reasons or to grant or withhold advance notice of its decision, as it sees fit. Although many businesses have acted in good faith to ease the impact of such decisions on their workers, once the decisions have been made, it is ques-

tionable how useful those efforts really are. The assistance offered consists largely of severance pay,
relocation pay, aid in finding a new job, and minimal
job retraining; rarely does it comprise all these elements. Even then it is inadequate to deal with the
tragic by-products of job losses and plant removals:
unemployment or income loss and underemploy-
ment, loss of family wealth, and deterioration of physical and mental health, as well as the creation of ghost
towns, community anomie, and related private and
public ills. (Barry Bluestone and Bennett Harrison,
*Capital and Communities: The Causes and Consequences
of Private Disinvestment*, Progressive Alliance, 1980,
pp. 62–83.)

The magnitude of the problem is staggering, as
is indicated by a 1987 report by the United States
General Accounting Office (GAO). (*Plant Closings/
Limited Advance Notice and Assistance Provided Dislocated
Workers*, GAO/HRD-87-105, July 1987.) It already had
in hand the results of a Bureau of Labor Statistics
(BLS) study, based on data obtained in the supple-
ment to the January 1986 Current Population Survey (CPS), which estimated that 10.8 million workers
20 years of age or older lost their jobs because of
closures or layoffs during the five-year period January 1981 to January 1986—an average of about 2.2
million workers a year. Although many of these dislocated workers were able to find new jobs, about
one-third were unemployed or no longer in the work
force when the January 1986 survey was conducted.
In addition, 38 percent of workers remained unemployed for more than six months following their dislocation. Older workers, women, and minorities were

less likely to be reemployed at the time of the CPS interview. Less than half of the dislocated workers age 55 or over were employed at the time of the BLS survey, whereas 72 percent of those under 55 were reemployed. About 57 percent of the minorities were working, compared to 68 percent of the dislocated nonminority workers. (*Ibid.*, p. 12.)

According to the GAO report, dislocated workers generally have a history of stable employment, with about one-third having job tenure of five years or more; yet they often are inadequately prepared to compete in the job market. In addition, according to the National Academy of Sciences, 20 to 30 percent of dislocated workers lack basic skills. Even when these workers are able to find new jobs, they may be unable to find work at wages or salaries comparable to what they formerly earned. Over 40 percent of the workers reemployed in full-time jobs earned less than in their prior jobs; for 30 percent, the wages at their new jobs were 20 percent or more below their previous wages. (*Ibid.*)

The report also took note of the serious impact a major closure or permanent layoff can have on a community. It found that the ripple effect of a major closure or layoff is often seen in the closure of small businesses or the loss of jobs dependent upon the closed establishment and the loss of the purchasing power of its workers. Property values often decline and the tax base erodes, leaving schools and other community services underfunded and unable to cope with the increased need for social welfare assistance for dislocated workers and their families. (*Ibid.*)

The GAO itself conducted a national survey of business establishments to determine the extent of business closures and permanent layoffs between January 1983 and December 1984, the length of advance notice provided to affected workers, and the assistance offered to dislocated workers by their employers. It reported that in 1983 and 1984 closures and permanent layoffs at about 16,200 establishments having 50 or more employees resulted in the dislocation of 1.3 million workers. Sixty percent of the closures and layoffs occurred in the manufacturing sector, reflecting long-term declines in many of these industries. Over one-third of the closures and layoffs occurred in industries adversely affected by foreign competition. A quarter million workers, however, were also dislocated from the fast-growing service sector. The GAO reported that although major business and labor organizations agree that, to be effective, employment assistance should be in place before dislocation occurs, few employers provided advance notice adequate to establish such programs. The median length of notice furnished to workers was seven days. About one-third of the establishments involved provided no notice before employment was terminated. When no union was present, over 40 percent of the establishments provided no notice to blue-collar workers. About one in seven employers offered workers a comprehensive assistance package composed of income maintenance, continued health insurance coverage, counseling, and job search assistance, but only 5 percent combined such assistance with more than 30 days' advance notice. (*Ibid.*, pp. 3–4, 35–36.)

B. Workers Adjustment and Retraining Notification Act

Congress responded to the growing demand that something be done to alleviate the plight of workers displaced by plant removals or closures or by mass permanent layoffs by passing the Worker Adjustment and Retraining Notification Act of 1988 (WARN). The Act became law without the signature of President Reagan, who had vigorously opposed it and had successfully vetoed an earlier version included in the Trade Bill. The original draft of the Act was substantially weakened by a series of compromises necessary to ensure its passage. The most that can be said for WARN is that it is a step in the right direction, but it affords only minimal, and grossly inadequate, protection to workers about to be displaced.

The heart of the new Act is Section 3, which provides that an employer shall not order a plant closing or mass layoff until the end of a 60-day period after the employer serves written notice of such order to the affected employees or their representatives, as well as to the state dislocated worker unit (designated or created under Title III of the Job Training Partnership Act) and the chief elected official of the unit of local government within which such closing or layoff is to occur. Under Section 5 of the Act, any employer who orders a plant closing or mass layoff in violation of Section 3 shall be liable to each aggrieved employee who suffers an "employment loss" (a term of art defined in the statute) as a result of such closing or layoff for back pay for each day of violation. Maximum liability is for 60 days, but in no event for more than one-half the number of days the employee was employed by the employer. Exclusive jurisdiction to enforce the Act is vested in the federal district courts, which, however, are expressly denied authority to enjoin a plant closing or mass layoff. Although the Secretary of Labor is empowered and directed to prescribe regulations to carry out the Act, including interpretive regulations describing the methods by which employers may provide for appropriate service of notice, he or she has no role to play in the enforcement of the Act.

A number of provisions of the new statute are designed to ease its impact on employers. One specifies that an employee may not be considered to have experienced an "employment loss" if the closing or layoff is the result of the relocation or consolidation of part or all of the employer's business and if prior to the closing or layoff the employer offers to transfer the employee to a different site of employment within a reasonable commuting distance with no more than a six-month break in employment, or the employer offers to transfer the employee to any other site of employment regardless of distance with no more than a six-month break in employment, and the employee accepts within a prescribed period.

Another provision permits an employer to shut down a single site of employment before the conclusion of the 60-day period if, as of the time the notice would have been required, "the employer was actively seeking capital or business which, if obtained, would have enabled the employer to avoid or postpone the shutdown and the employer reasonably and in good faith believed that giving the notice required would have precluded the employer from obtaining the needed capital or business." An employer may also order a plant closing or mass layoff before the conclusion of the 60-day period "if the closing or mass layoff is caused by business circumstances that were not reasonably foreseeable as of the time notice would have been required." Similarly, a layoff of more than six months that, at its outset, was announced to be of six months or less will be treated as an "employment loss" unless "the extension beyond six months is caused by business circumstances (including unforeseeable changes in price or cost) not reasonably foreseeable at the time of the initial layoff" and notice is given at the time it becomes "reasonably foreseeable" that the extension beyond six months will be required.

Still another provision exempts from coverage under the Act the closing of a temporary facility or a closing or layoff resulting from the completion of a particular project for which the affected employees were hired with the understanding that their employment was limited to the duration of the project; the same provision also exempts a closing or layoff constituting a lockout under the National Labor Relations Act not intended to evade the requirements of WARN.

Finally, the Act provides for reduction of an employer's liability for violation of its terms, at the discretion of the court, if the employer proves to the satisfaction of the court that the violation was in good faith and that the employer had reasonable grounds for believing that it had not committed a violation.

The prognosis for the prompt and vigorous enforcement of WARN is not good. The Act abounds
with ambiguous terms and provisions, the meaning
and application of each of which will be vigorously
litigated by the affected parties. Employers, in particular, have announced their intention to prove that
their dire predictions as to the effects the new law
would have on their ability to conduct their businesses in an efficient manner were correct. The Department of Labor has issued an "Interpretive Rule" (54
F.R. 16042, April 20, 1989) that has been attacked in
some respects by all the affected parties. The outlook
is thus for protracted litigation in the courts before
authoritative interpretations of disputed provisions
of the Act can be established. Moreover, given the
mood of organized business, it is doubtful that the
pitifully short 60-day notice period will be used for
what it was intended, that is, a time for management
to explore with workers or their representatives the
alternatives to closing or layoff and to set in motion
various schemes to ease the shock of displacement,
should it occur. One can only hope that Congress
will keep its eye on the problem and will adopt
stronger measures to deal with it as the inadequa-
cies of the present legislation become increasingly
apparent.

C. Mergers, Takeovers, and Leveraged Buyouts

Particularly during the last decade, there has been
an unprecedented rise in the number of corporate
mergers, takeovers, and leveraged buyouts. These re-
structurings, in which equity is replaced with massive

amounts of debt, have had a severe impact on the affected workers. AFL-CIO President Lane Kirkland testified before the Senate Banking Committee in January 1989 that as many as 90,000 union members have lost jobs and that thousands more have been forced to take wage and benefits cuts over the past decade. He charged that the debt resulting from these transactions

> "is assumed not for the purpose of industrial expansion or increased competitiveness, but as a stock market manipulation ploy which serves little purpose other than to line the pockets of speculators with fast-earned mega-profits, as well as their investment bankers and their lawyers with fees running into the millions." (BNA *Daily Labor Report*, No. 17, Jan. 27, 1989, p. A-5.)

He added that employees of these companies are frequently placed at great risk, "while billions of dollars are channelled into the hands that neither create nor produce goods or services." (*Ibid.*)

I am aware of counterarguments to the effect that, on the whole, the mergers, takeovers, and leveraged buyouts have made for a more efficient economy, but I am convinced that present laws permit many abuses of the system. Whether the appropriate remedy is that urged by Kirkland and others—disallowance as tax deductions of debt to finance a leveraged buyout, a takeover, or the retirement of equity—is a matter for consideration by the experts. What must be taken into account, however, is the effect of such transactions on the working lives of the employees involved.

Such an approach is illustrated by a recently enacted Massachusetts statute that delays any hostile takeover for three years once the bidder has obtained 5 percent of the company's stock. The acquisition will be allowed to proceed only if the combination is approved by two-thirds of the shareholders or if the raider is able to acquire 90 percent of the firm's stock. In addition, the law requires the acquiring company to provide two weeks' severance pay for each year of employment to workers laid off within two years after the firm changes hands. The corporation formed as the result of the takeover will also be required to assume existing collective bargaining agreements. These labor provisions apply to any company engaging in a takeover in which a Massachusetts firm employing more than 50 full-time workers is involved, even if the firm being acquired is not incorporated in Massachusetts. The legislation also explicitly states that the corporate directors may consider the interests of the work force, the community, and other parties, in addition to those of the shareholders, when deciding on the best course of action. (BNA, *Daily Labor Report*, No. 137, July 19, 1989, pp. A-5–A-6.)

In one respect, the Massachusetts statute is incompatible with existing case law under the National Labor Relations Act, which holds that although a successor employer may have a duty to bargain with an existing union, it does not have to observe the substantive terms of a collective bargaining agreement between that union and the predecessor employer.

(*NLRB v. Burns International Security Services*, 406 U.S.
272 [1972].) The *Burns* case illustrates the Supreme
Court's concern about protecting the mobility of capital, a mobility that the Court obviously thought
would be inhibited if successor employers were subject to terms and conditions of employment nego-
tiated by their predecessors. The double standard
existing in this regard is apparent, however, when
we consider the common corporate practice of prom-
ising "golden parachutes" to executives who may lose
their jobs in a corporate takeover or merger. Those
payments presumably exercise some deterrent effect
on acquiring companies, but they are nevertheless
perfectly legal.

Unions have been joined by public interest groups
in calling for protection for employee and retiree
pension and health benefits in leveraged buyout
situations. According to estimates of the House
Education and Labor Subcommittee on Labor-
Management Relations, pension plan assets currently
stand at approximately $2 trillion and pension plans
contain approximately $100 billion more than is
needed to pay pension obligations. Since 1980, approximately 2,000 defined benefit plans have been
terminated. (BNA *Daily Labor Report*, No. 41, March
3, 1989, p. A-5.) The termination of a pension plan
and the reversion of excess funds to the acquiring
employer frequently leave the employees of the
predecessor company without any protection other
than those limited pension rights that have already
vested. The American Association of Retired Persons
has recommended legislative action to discourage

reversions by requiring that a share of the reversion assets go to employees and retirees, requiring a "cushion" in any newly established plan, increasing excise taxes on reversions, and prohibiting asset reversions in takeover activity. (*Ibid.*) Again, although such proposals may be insufficient to solve all the problems involved in leveraged buyouts and may even be more drastic than is prudent or necessary, they focus attention on the harm such transactions do to workers and their equity.

My point is simply that employees of an acquired company are not merely bloodless assets or liabilities; they are human beings who often have given years of dedicated service to the predecessor employer and whose welfare and prospects ought to be an important element in the calculus of the takeover. If, as is too often the case, their interests are completely ignored in the free exercise of market forces, government has a duty to provide minimum protection of those interests in the form of notice and benefits guarantees.

Conditions of Employment

A. *Industrial Homework and Child Labor*

Industrial homework has historically been characterized by exploitation of the workers involved, especially women and children. It was banned in seven apparel industries in 1942, after the Department of Labor found that it could not otherwise enforce the provisions of the Fair Labor Standards Act of 1938 in those industries. Under prodding from the Reagan administration, however, the Department lifted the ban in the knitted outerwear industry in 1984, and in January 1989 it lifted it in five other industries: nonhazardous jewelry manufacturing, gloves and mittens, button and buckle manufacturing, handkerchief manufacturing, and embroideries. The earlier action was opposed by a number of union and industry officials, state and federal officials, and various other public figures, including former Secretaries of Labor Arthur Goldberg, Willard Wirtz, and Ray Marshall and former Wage and Hours Administrator Clarence Lundquist. The chief objections were the difficulty of locating and identifying homework employers and their homeworkers, the inordinate amount of time required to conduct investigations of employers having homeworkers, and the difficulty of restoring back wages to homeworkers paid in violation of the FLSA. (U. S. Department of Labor, "Industrial Homework in Knitted Outerwear Industry," 49 *Federal Register* 44262.) The rule change for the smaller industries is being opposed by the International Ladies' Garment Workers Union (ILGWU) and others, who contend that the Department of Labor's new enforcement measures (through a certification procedure) still preclude meaningful FLSA enforcement. They have brought a suit against the Department that is pending in the Federal District Court for the District of Columbia.

At hearings conducted by the Department of Labor, a witness representing the Pennsylvania Department of Labor and Industry stated that removing the ban on homework "exposes the poorest and most vulnerable members of society to exploitation and unacceptable dangers." He questioned whether it would be possible to ensure that workers receive the minimum wage, to protect children from the violations of child labor laws, and to police homeworking establishments if the ban is lifted. The president of the ILGWU testified that industrial homework, legal or not, almost always violates many local health, fire, and building laws. The Attorney General of New York emphasized that homework remains a danger to people's lives as well as to workers' rights. "Homeworkers are still subjected to long hours, subminimum wages, and illegal deductions from their pay," he stated. "They are forced to enlist the help of their children to meet impossible deadlines," he continued, "and children are subjected to the risk of injury from sewing machines, hot irons and presses, sharp scissors, and small objects—like pins, needles, and buttons—that litter the homeworker's living room." Finally, a professor of community medicine and pediatrics at the Mt. Sinai School of Medicine in New York testified that besides the "chronic fatigue, the blighted childhood, the lost education, and the perpetuation of the cycle of family poverty that result from employment of children in industrial homework," children are either directly or indirectly exposed to toxic materials, such as formaldehyde, a known carcinogen, which vaporizes from permanent press fabric. (BNA, *Daily Labor Report*, No. 63, April 4, 1989, p. A-9.)

Because the work force in the apparel industry has a large component of immigrants, primarily Asian and Hispanic, who are particularly at risk economically, and because the industry must compete directly with foreign apparel producers, many of whom have no obligation to provide even minimally humane employment standards, the number of sweatshops has sharply increased. Senator Bill Bradley testified that in July 1988 there were about 30,000 persons working in at least 1,500 sweatshops in New Jersey alone. (*Ibid.*, p. A-10.)

More recently, a GAO study revealed that the majority of the approximately 7,000 apparel firms in New York City are operated under sweatshop conditions in which federal, state, and city labor laws are routinely violated. The study cited the estimate of the New York State Labor Department that about 4,500 of the state's apparel firms fell into this category and that about 50,000 workers, including many Hispanic and Asian illegal immigrants, are employed by apparel firms that have a history of violating federal, state, and local labor laws on a regular basis. According to the GAO, the enforcement pattern in New York City is similar to the pattern nationwide. Efforts to regulate multiple labor law violators, the study reported, are limited by "insufficient staff resources, inadequate penalties for violation of federal wage and hour statutes, and limited coordination among enforcement agencies." (*"Sweatshops" in New York City: A Local Example of a Nationwide Problem*, GAO/HRD-89-101 BR, 1989, *passim.*)

The conditions revealed by these data are reminiscent of the early years of the Industrial Revolution; certainly, they are unacceptable today. The Department of Labor's certification procedures are simply inadequate to screen out violators of the FLSA, and it lacks the personnel and the commitment to enforce vigorously the maximum hours, minimum wages, and child labor restrictions of that statute in the industries from which it proposes to lift the ban against industrial homework. Surely a country as prosperous as the United States need not tolerate, in the name of "competitiveness," this egregious exploitation of men, women, and children that results from legalized industrial homework.

B. Family and Medical Leave

The United States is the only industrial country with no national parental leave policy. Almost every country in the world, including our most successful economic competitors in Western Europe and Asia, has a compulsory parental leave policy. Most impose requirements that go beyond what is being proposed for this country. In Europe, for example, 5 to 6 months of paid leave is the norm for new mothers. Even Japan, which often lags behind European labor standards, provides 12 to 14 weeks of partially paid maternity leave with full job guarantees. (Report of the Senate Committee on Labor and Human Resources on Family and Medical Leave Act of 1989, 101 Cong., 1st Sess, 1989, S. 345, p. 24.)

The majority of American families today are comprised of two-earner couples both members of which work outside the home. More than one-half of all mothers with infants under one year of age work outside the home. At present, women constitute 45 percent of the work force, and by 1990 their work force

participation is expected to rise to at least 50 percent. Moreover, 56 percent of American women are
now in the work force, and 80 percent of these are
in their prime childbearing years. According to the
BLS, 90 percent of fathers and more than 60 percent
of mothers are working outside the home. The new
economic reality is that today's families depend upon
a woman's income to survive. Two out of every three
women working outside the home are either the sole
providers for their children or have husbands who
earn less than $15,000 per year. Women are the sole
parent in 16 percent of all families. In March 1988
approximately 13 million children, about one-fifth
of all American children, were living in more than
7.7 million single-parent families. Nearly 6.7 million
of these families were headed by mothers. (*Ibid.*,
p. 23.)

   Many new parents have no guarantee that their
jobs will be protected either when they are unable
to work due to pregnancy, childbirth, or related medical conditions or after childbirth, adoption, or foster
care, when they need to stay at home to care for their
infants. In the absence of a family leave standard,
childbirth and the need to care for a sick child or
parent have an adverse impact on women's earnings.
According to a 1988 study by the Institute for Wom-
en's Policy Research, by the year after giving birth,
the earnings of mothers were $1.40 per hour lower
than those of women who did not give birth (although the former's earnings had been higher before
birth). The researchers attributed much of this earnings loss to the lack of job protection for the new

mothers. Adoptive parents also face difficulties in the absence of a reasonable family leave policy. Most adoption agencies require the presence of a parent in the home—some for as long as four months— when a child is placed with a family. (*Ibid.*, pp. 24–25.)

Child development and medical specialists have stressed the importance of infant-parent bonding during the first few months of a child's life and of the value of the almost continuous presence at the hospital of a parent of a seriously ill child. Yet if a parent loses his or her job because he or she chooses to remain at home or at the hospital, critical medical insurance may be forfeited. Similar problems arise when a worker must deal with the serious illness of a parent or simply provide care for the elderly. Approximately 7 million workers care for the elderly, with more than one-third of that number caring for their parents. Three out of every four caregivers are women, and nearly one out of three is poor. In 1987, there were 27 million noninstitutionalized elderly in the United States, with the elderly segment growing faster than the rest of the population. This trend, coupled with the steady increase of women in the work force, points to the critical need for policies that accommodate caregiving for the worker's parent. (*Ibid.*, pp. 26–28.)

Existing family leave policies fall far short of meeting the needs of today's workers. Although many employers do permit some type of leave under limited circumstances, a large proportion of employers have yet to adopt such policies. Most limit their leave policies to the immediate period of physical disability related to childbirth. Many women are covered by

such maternity-as-disability leave, but the duration
and job protections vary widely, and "bonding" leave
for infant care after disability is much more limited. Leave for fathers and for adoption is rarely available, and leave for a child's or elderly parent's serious
illness is unusual. A 1988 study reported that only
16 percent of employers have an ill-child leave policy, and only 14 percent have an ill-parent policy.
Whether health insurance coverage is continued during leave varies widely among employers. Moreover,
there are indications that the availability and the
scope of current family leave policies are severely
limited for those in lower-paying jobs. This problem
is compounded by the fact that these workers are less
able financially to deal with family crises. Management and professional employees are more likely
than blue-collar workers to receive employer contributions to health insurance during maternity disability leave, for example.

   In addition to family leave, there is a need for unpaid job-protected leave and the continuation of any
existing health insurance coverage during a worker's
serious illness. The rationale for such a policy is that
it is unfair and possibly catastrophic for a worker to
be terminated when he or she succumbs to a serious
illness and is incapable of working. Medical leave is
now a necessity for American workers, especially for
poor ones with families. The urgent need for such
leave was eloquently stated by Eleanor Holmes Nor-
ton in her testimony before the Senate committee:

"For the single parent, usually a woman, losing her job when she is unable to work during a time of serious health conditions . . . can often mean borrowing beyond prudence, going on welfare, or destitution for herself and her family. Indeed, it is hard to understand how single parents, who have no choice but to work to support their families, have survived under the present system. For this highly vulnerable group, whose numbers have exploded, a job guarantee for periods when they or their children have serious health conditions is urgently necessary. The high rates of single parenthood among minority families and of labor force participation by minority single mothers make job-guaranteed leaves especially critical for minorities." (*Ibid.*, p. 31.)

In response to these various pressing problems, both the House and the Senate are considering proposed bills designed to ameliorate them. S. 345, the Family and Medical Leave Act of 1989, provides for 10 weeks of unpaid family leave during any 24-month period to workers for the birth, adoption, or serious illness of a worker's son or daughter or for the serious illness of the worker's parent. A worker unable to perform the functions of his or her position because of serious ill health is entitled to temporary unpaid medical leave not to exceed 13 weeks during any 12-month period. S. 345 covers employers who employ 20 or more employees at any one work site for each working day during 20 or more calendar weeks in the current or preceding calendar year. To be eligible for leave, a worker must have been

employed by that employer for 12 months and for
not less than 900 hours.

During family or medical leave, the worker's preex-
isting health benefits must be maintained. The employer is under no obligation to accrue seniority or
other employment benefits for the absent worker
during the leave period. Upon return from leave, the
worker must be restored to the same position he or
she left or to an equivalent position. The taking of
leave may not result in the loss of any benefit earned
before the leave, nor may it entitle the worker to any
right or benefit other than that to which he or she
was entitled on the date the leave commenced.

It is estimated that S. 345 covers 12 percent of
U. S. employers and 47 percent of U. S. workers.

Title II of S. 345 extends coverage to federal civil
service employees. Title III establishes a bipartisan
Commission on Family and Medical Leave for the
purpose of conducting a comprehensive study of existing and proposed policies relating to family and
medical leave and the potential benefits and costs
of such policies for employers. The Commission is
to report its findings to Congress within two years
from the date it first meets.

The GAO projected the impact of the proposed
legislation on employers presently without family
leave policies. According to its analysis, S. 345 will
have no measurable effect on work place routines
or productivity. After an intensive survey of 80 firms
with leave policies in two metropolitan labor markets, the GAO found that only 30 percent of workers
taking leave are replaced. Instead, employers tend

to reallocate the work of those on leave to other workers. The GAO also found that the cost of replacement
workers is generally similar to or less than the cost
of the worker replaced and that employers believe
the use of a replacement does not result in a significant loss of output. On the basis of this survey, the
GAO estimated that S. 345 would result in fewer than
one in 275 workers being absent from work at any
one time. Accordingly, the GAO concluded that
"there will be little, if any, measurable net costs to
employers associated with a firm's method of adjusting to workers taking leave under this proposal."
(*Ibid.*, p. 34.) The cost of the proposed legislation
would result exclusively from the continuation of
health insurance for employees on unpaid leave. The
GAO estimates that for employers, the annual cost
per covered employee would average $4.35. The to-
tal cost of the proposed legislation would come to
$236 million. (*Ibid.*)

Opponents of S. 345 and similar bills argue that
a national leave policy of the type those bills establish would reduce overall employee benefits because
employers would be forced to eliminate voluntary
benefits in order to pay for the new family and medical leave requirements, would burden small businesses with the costs of compulsory leave regardless
of their ability to absorb such costs, and would create a vast new federal bureaucracy to administer and
enforce the new leave policy.

It is not clear at this writing whether S. 345 or the
comparable House bill, H.R. 770, will be enacted or
whether, should a bill be passed, it will be signed or
vetoed by President Bush. There are few matters on

the national agenda, however, of greater urgency and importance. Sooner or later, legislation such as S. 345 and H.R. 770 is almost certain to be enacted, because the need for it is so widespread and pressing. One way, therefore, to help establish a "kinder and gentler" society is to adopt appropriate legislation at the earliest possible time.

Administration of Laws Affecting Employment

During the Reagan administration, unions complained of a prevailing attitude of indifference or open hostility on the part of various executive and administrative agencies, such as the Department of Labor and the National Labor Relations Board (NRLB), in the enforcement of labor laws. NLRB policies and procedures came under increasing criticism by some of the nation's leading labor law experts. (Perhaps the most notable example is Paul C. Weiler, "Promises to Keep: Securing Workers' Rights to Self-Organization Under the NLRA," 96 *Harvard Law Review*, 1983, pp. 1769–1827.) There were also continuing charges of laxness by the Department of Labor in its administration of the Occupational Safety and Health Act of 1970.

A detailed analysis and evaluation of these charges is beyond the purview of this paper. It is sufficient to note that, for whatever reasons, unions and the workers they represent have lost faith in the capacity or willingness of various government agencies to enforce the labor laws vigorously and evenhandedly. This disaffection has now extended to decisions of the Supreme Court, which is currently dominated by Reagan appointees, in the area of employment discrimination. I propose to examine just three of those decisions and to show why, in my judgment, the widespread feeling of dismay they have engendered is entirely justified.

Beginning with the Court's landmark decision in 1954, in *Brown v. Board of Education* (347 U.S. 483), and continuing during the next two decades, which saw the enactment of Title VII of the Civil Rights Act of 1964 (CRA) (42 U.S.C. Sections 2000e –2000e-17), prohibiting employment discrimination based on race, religion, sex, and national origin, there developed a strong legislative policy against employment discrimination in all its forms. This policy received decisive support in a unanimous 1971 decision by the Supreme Court in *Griggs v. Duke Power Co.* (401 U.S. 424.) In that case the Court held that Title VII of the CRA prohibits, in addition to intentional discrimination, employment practices which, while neutral on their face, are statistically shown to have a discriminatory impact on minorities that is unrelated to job performance. This phenomenon came to be known by the shorthand term "disparate impact." The rule established in *Griggs* and in later cases required that the plaintiff bear the burden of showing that an employer's job practices had a disparate impact on minorities or women. The employer then had the burden of establishing a business necessity for the practices by showing that they were related to the successful performance of the job in question. Even if the employer was able to make such a showing, however, the plaintiff could still prevail by demonstrating that other equally predictive practices having a less disparate impact were available to the employer.

In *Wards Cove Packing Co. v. Atonio* (109 S. Ct. 2115 [1989]), the Supreme Court turned 18 years of solid precedent upside down. The case arose in an Alaskan salmon cannery. It involved unskilled, low-paying cannery jobs, filled largely by nonwhites, and both skilled and unskilled higher-paying noncannery jobs, filled largely by whites. The plaintiffs were nonwhites who alleged that various of the employer's hiring and promotions practices were responsible for racial stratification of the work force and had denied them employment as noncannery workers on the basis of race. The Court majority of five Justices held, among other things, that the ultimate burden of proof was on the plaintiffs, not the employer, including the extremely difficult burden of proving the specific employment practice that had caused the disparate impact. Moreover, the Court majority stated that when a number of employment practices are alleged to have combined to create a disparate impact, the plaintiffs must demonstrate the statistical disparity created by each challenged practice. The Court also reduced the burden of proof on employers. It declared that an employer's justification for the disparate impact need not be "business necessity" but could be simply "legitimate employment goals"; moreover, the employer's burden is now merely one of production of evidence, not of persuasion. Plaintiffs, to be sure, still have the opportunity to prevail by demonstrating that other employment practices that did not have such a discriminatory effect were available to the employer. Nevertheless, the Court majority emphasized that any alternative practices must be equally as effective as those challenged.

The net result of this decision is that the employer's burden in a disparate impact case is now virtually identical to that in an intentional discrimination case; that is, it need only articulate a legitimate, non-discriminatory reason for its challenged conduct. That is not what the Court has been saying for the past 18 years and almost certainly is not what Congress intended. One can only echo the words of Justice Stevens in dissent:

"Turning a blind eye to the meaning and purpose of Title VII, the majority's opinion perfunctorily rejects a longstanding rule of law and underestimates the probative value of evidence of a racially stratified workforce. I cannot join this latest sojourn into judicial activism." (*Ibid.*, p. 2127–2128.)

In *Patterson v. McLean Credit Union* (109 S. Ct. 2363 [1989]), the Supreme Court, again by a 5-to-4 decision, virtually eliminated the Civil Rights Act of 1866 (42 U.S.C. Section 1981) as a source of protection against employment discrimination in the private sector. Section 1981 prohibits racial discrimination in connection with the making and enforcement of contractual rights. In 1976, in *Runyon v. McCrary* (427 U.S. 160), the Court held that Section 1981 applies to racial discrimination in the private sector. *Patterson* involved a cause of action for racial harassment by an employer. The Court declined to reverse *Runyon* but sharply restricted its application by holding that Section 1981 covers only conduct at the initial formation of a contract (hiring or promotion) and conduct that impairs a person's ability to use the legal process to enforce that contract; working conditions and breaches of the contract are not covered.

The effect of this decision is to deprive approximately 15 percent of workers in the private sector of any protection against racial discrimination, because they work for employers who have fewer than fifteen workers and are therefore not covered by Title VII of the CRA. Moreover, Section 1981 provides remedies not available under Title VII. It has no coverage limits, no requirement of administrative exhaustion, a longer filing period, and the availability of punitive damages. In the years since *Runyon* was decided, Section 1981 had become a counterpart to Title VII in racial discrimination in employment cases, because Congress had expressly provided that the remedies provided by Title VII are not exclusive. Now the Court has virtually eliminated Section 1981 as a source of relief in such cases.

I find it impossible to understand the reasoning of the court majority in *Patterson*. The plaintiff had alleged that she had been subject to various acts of racial harassment during her employment. "This type of conduct," said Justice Kennedy for the Court majority, "reprehensible though it may be if true, is not actionable under § 1981, which covers only conduct at the initial formation of the contract and conduct which impairs the right to enforce contract obligations through legal process." (*Ibid.*, p. 2374.) Certainly, a worker is deprived of the benefits of an employment contract if he or she is subjected to acts of racial discrimination under that contract with no possibility of relief. Theoretically, the plaintiff could have sued for relief from racial harassment under Title VII, but for those not covered by Title VII there is now no relief. And what sort of sense or justice does it make to say that racial discrimination is barred in making contracts of employment, but once the contract is made, the worker may be discriminated against with respect to terms of employment and subjected to various forms of racial harassment without there being any violation of Section 1981?

Nor is it an answer to say that relief is available to the injured worker under state laws. Most states continue to apply the common-law doctrine of "employment at will," under which an employer can dismiss a worker for any reason or no reason at any time. Unless the employer has adopted a specific policy against racial harassment, it is doubtful that it can be sued for such discrimination under state law for breach of contract.

In summary, it seems to me obvious that the language of Section 1981—"All persons shall have the same right . . . to make and enforce contracts . . . as is enjoyed by white citizens"—encompasses a worker's right to protection from racial harassment by his or her employer. While purporting to preserve *Runyon* on the ground of *stare decisis*, the Court has sapped that decision of most of its vitality. It would have been more honest simply to have overruled that precedent.

Finally, I want to refer to the Supreme Court's decision weakening the effects of voluntary affirmative action hiring and promotion plans. These plans have been increasingly common in Title VII litigation, and many hundreds of decrees approving and establishing such plans have been issued by federal district courts. The usual parties to the litigation producing the consent decrees are minority or female workers and employers; the typical majority group consisting of white males is normally not a party.

In *Martin v. Wilks* (109 S. Ct. 2180 [1989]), another 5-to-4 decision, the Supreme Court held that white plaintiffs claiming to be victims of reverse discrimination may challenge the impact upon them of consent decrees, including goals for hiring and promoting black firefighters in Birmingham, Alabama, so long as the plaintiffs were not participants in the proceedings in which the decrees were entered. The white group, which was aware of the original litigation but chose not to intervene, was thus allowed, years later, collaterally to challenge the validity of the decree in an independent Title VII suit claiming that its application was discriminatory as to them. A majority of the federal courts of appeals had held that such collateral attacks were impermissible, on the grounds that they would discourage voluntary settlement of discrimination claims, and that white groups who had knowledge of the litigation but chose not to intervene were estopped from attacking the decree after entry. This doctrine was rejected by the Supreme Court.

The immediate effect of *Martin* is to discourage employers from entering into consent decrees involving affirmative action; the risk is too great that somewhere down the line the decree will be collaterally attacked by those persons who were not parties to it. The ramifications of the decision, however, are much broader. In *United Steelworkers v. Weber* (443 U.S. 193 [1979]), the Court held that a voluntary affirmative action plan is lawful if it is designed to eliminate a conspicuous imbalance in a traditionally segregated job category, is temporary, and does not unnecessarily trammel the rights of nonminority workers. Subsequently, many consent decrees were based on the belief that, under *Weber*, voluntary affirmative action plans are permissible. If those decrees are now subject to collateral attack, the issue whether such plans are permissible under Title VII may again be raised, with the possibility that the Supreme Court, as presently constituted, might very well overrule *Weber*.

Similar problems exist with respect to minority "set-asides" in government programs. In *Fullilove v. Klutznick* (448 U.S. 448 [1980]), the Supreme Court held that a minority business enterprise provision of a federal construction grant program to state and local governments, requiring 10 percent of the business performed under the grant to be set aside for entities owned by racial and ethnic minority persons, is constitutionally valid. A number of consent decrees were issued on the strength of that decision. Now, in *City of Richmond v. Croson* (109 S. Ct. 706 [1989]), decided in January 1989, the Supreme Court has ruled that a city's 30 percent minority contract set-aside program was unconstitutional because it was not justified by a compelling government interest and was not narrowly tailored to accomplish a remedial purpose. Thus, there is a good possibility that previous consent decrees based on *Fullilove* will now be reconsidered and vacated.

Affirmative action has been an indispensable part of the national commitment to abolish employment discrimination in its various forms. In its recent decisions, some of which I have not discussed here, the Supreme Court has seriously undermined the legitimacy of affirmative action and has delivered a disturbing setback to the civil rights movement in general. This is hardly the way to create a "kinder and gentler" society. The new Court majority, made up largely of Reagan appointees, seems likely to hold sway for some time to come. The only way to combat its retrograde employment discrimination decisions is through appropriate federal legislation.

Conclusion

Getting and holding a job in this country today is for millions of men and women a desperate and often hopeless endeavor. Increasingly, new entrants into the labor force lack the basic skills necessary to perform the jobs that are available. This situation reflects a basic inadequacy in our system of public education, aggravated by the alarming number of high school dropouts, particularly in our big cities. Most of those persons who are employed in entry-level jobs are not receiving the training needed to upgrade their skills and make them eligible for higher-paying work. Even some workers in semi-

skilled or skilled jobs face an uncertain future, as employers reduce wages and benefits and introduce
labor-saving technology in an effort to compete successfully with goods produced in Third World countries with much lower labor standards. Increasingly
in recent years, companies have simply moved their
operations abroad, leaving in their wake unemployed
domestic workers and disrupted communities.

Seeking remedies for these problems is like tear-
ing a seamless web: It is difficult to know how best
to attack them and at what point. Hard as it is, I think
we must start by trying to salvage as many young
people—the next generation of workers—as we can.
Because an ever-growing proportion of them are
black or Hispanic, this means that we must do what
we can to improve the quality of their lives, for example, by providing better housing and health care,
helping to preserve family units, and seeking to rid
their neighborhoods of gang violence and drugs.
These are not easy tasks and there is no likelihood
that they will be accomplished in the immediate future, but we must make a start.

In the schools, greater emphasis should be placed
on teaching those basic skills, such as effective use
of the English language and mathematics, that equip
students to learn a variety of tasks and to deal with
change. Workers today can look forward to the need
to learn how to perform a number of different jobs
during their lifetimes, and they must be able to cope
with these challenges. We must also step up our efforts to steer young men and women away from
drugs and to cut down on the number of teen preg-
nancies—two major causes of high school dropouts.

Although we have made considerable progress in stamping out the more overt and egregious forms of employment discrimination, we still have a long way to go before we are finally rid of racism and sexism in our society. The recent decisions of the Supreme Court to which I have adverted are roadblocks in our path toward that goal. Realistically, these can be overcome only by legislation affirming Congress's commitment to affirmative action and to the elimination of employment practices that have a disparate impact on racial and ethnic minorities and women.

Indeed, most of the solutions to the problems I have discussed are legislative. We need laws to increase the minimum wage; to provide workers with some protection against plant closures, removals, mass permanent layoffs, mergers, takeovers, and leveraged buyouts; and to provide for family and medical leaves. Of course, all this costs money—lots of it. The issue is one of national priorities. We have to decide, for example, whether we want to buy a 100 billion-dollar Stealth bombers or put that money into one or more of the social programs I have mentioned. Over and above the juggling of existing budgets for defense and other purposes, we must make up our minds whether the problems I have outlined are sufficiently pressing to warrant tax increases to help in their elimination or amelioration. This is a great country and a rich country. If we are determined to bring about a "kinder and gentler" society, we can eventually do so, but we must be prepared to postpone less urgent goals and to make some economic sacrifices. The time to act is now: Let us resolve to transform President Bush's statement of national purpose from a mere rhetorical flourish into a determined program of reform.

EQUALITY

by

Andrew R. Cecil

Andrew R. Cecil

Andrew R. Cecil is Distinguished Scholar in Residence at The University of Texas at Dallas. In February 1979 the University established in his honor the Andrew R. Cecil Lectures on Moral Values in a Free Society and invited Dr. Cecil to deliver the first series of lectures in November 1979. The first annual proceedings were published as Dr. Cecil's book The Third Way: Enlightened Capitalism and the Search for a New Social Order, *which received an enthusiastic response. He has also lectured in each subsequent series. A new book,* The Foundations of a Free Society, *was published in 1983. Another,* Three Sources of National Strength, *appeared in 1986.* Equality, Tolerance and Liberty *was published in 1990. In 1976, the University named for Dr. Cecil the Andrew R. Cecil Auditorium in his honor.*

Educated in Europe and well launched on a career as a professor and practitioner in the fields of law and economics, Dr. Cecil resumed his academic career after World War II in Lima, Peru, at the University of San Marcos. After 1949, he was associated with the Methodist church-affiliated colleges and universities in the United States until he joined The Southwestern Legal Foundation. Associated with the Foundation since 1958, Dr. Cecil helped guide its development of five educational centers that offer nationally and internationally recognized programs in advanced continuing education. Since his retirement as President of the Foundation, he serves as Chancellor Emeritus and Honorary Trustee.

Dr. Cecil is author of fifteen books on the subjects of law, economics, and religion and of more than seventy articles on these subjects and on the philosophy of religion published in periodicals and anthologies. A member of the American Society of International Law, of the American Branch of the International Law Association, and of the American Judicature Society, Dr. Cecil has served on numerous commissions for the Methodist Church and is a member of the Board of Trustees of the National Methodist Foundation for Christian Higher Education. In 1981 he was named an Honorary Rotarian.

EQUALITY
by
Andrew R. Cecil

The Idea of Equality

The famous watchwords of the French Revolution —*"Liberté, égalité, fraternité"*—became the rallying cry not only of that revolution itself but of many subsequent generations of liberals and reformers the world over. Among the three ideals of liberty, equality, and brotherhood, the goal of equality has the most complex ramifications in mankind's quest to implement it. Equality has become a byword. The history of mankind can be seen as the history of an increasing passion for equality, and the rise of democratic forms of governance reflects the putting into practice of the operative ideals of liberty and equality.

All men desire to be free and to be respected. This invincible passion for equality can prevail in either of two ways: It can lift the weak up to the level of the strong, or it can drag the strong down to the level of the weak. Poor or disenfranchised people want to be elevated to the rank of the powerful. If they fail in this, their disappointment may induce them to prefer equality in slavery, where rights are given to nobody, to humiliating inequality. Thus it has happened that people's instinctive taste for equality has ignited bloody revolutions that, when they missed their mark, have given birth to emperors and dictators.

191

A. *Greece*

The idea of equality has preoccupied the minds of many great thinkers since the ancient philosophers of Greece and Rome and the Hebrew prophets. In Greece, the good life—which was the object of all philosophical inquiry and political activity—was offered only to free individuals. Aristotle, for instance, contemptuously regarded slaves as "living tools." His concept that "equality consists in the same treatment of similar persons" was compatible with the existence of many unequal groups in the Greek polity, where women, aliens, slaves, mechanics, tradesmen, and husbandmen were excluded from the equal possession of liberty enjoyed by free citizens.

In stating that "everywhere inequality is a cause of revolution," Aristotle pointed out that disputes arise "when persons who are not equal receive equal shares." He found the very "springs and fountains of revolution" in the faulty notions concerning equality held by those who advocated democracy and oligarchy. The democrats claimed that since men should be equally free, they should be absolutely equal in all respects. The oligarchs advocated the idea that those who are unequal in one respect are unequal in all respects. The absolute standards that these two forms of government offer, according to Aristotle, "stir up revolution."

In *The Republic*, Plato described the ideal state, to be ruled by philosophers, where private property and family will be abolished and education will fit each for his part in the common life. He was not much interested in equality. In one of his discussions related to the relative equality of the sexes, Plato reached the conclusion that the gifts of nature are alike diffused in men and women; therefore all the pursuits of men are the pursuits of women also, "but in all of them a woman is inferior to a man." Aristotle and Plato accepted the class structure in the Greek city-state as a perfect social organization written in the eternal and final order of political life.

Pericles, the Athenian statesman and one of the greatest patrons of the arts, advanced democracy in Athens through various steps. Among these was the opening of every office to any citizen. The idea of equality was a part of his political leadership. In the celebrated funeral oration made at the end of the first year of the Peloponnesian War (which began in 431 B.C.), Pericles made a strong appeal to the pride and patriotism of the citizens and stressed the importance of equality as the noblest expression of Athenian democracy:

"If we look to the laws, they afford equal justice to all in their private differences; if to social standing, advancement in public life falls to reputation for capacity, class consideration not being allowed to interfere with merit; nor again does poverty bar the way—if a man is able to serve the state, he is not hindered by the obscurity of his condition. The freedom which we enjoy in our government extends also to our ordinary life."

Somewhat later in the development of Greek thought, the school of the Stoics, which formulated its philosophy in the third and second centuries B.C., advocated the equality of all human beings. The Stoics identified reason with God, and because of each person's ability to reason, they attributed to each a spark of divinity. Slavery, they argued, rejects or denies this fragment of divinity and therefore should be abolished. In contrast to Aristotle and Plato they stressed the resemblance, rather than the differences, among human beings, as well as the unity of mankind bound by universal law. Under this law, they claimed, all human beings are equal.

B. Rome

The Roman philosophers adopted this stoic conception of natural law. The Roman dramatist and statesman Lucius Annaeus Seneca observed that the "world is the one parent of all." Cicero, the Roman politician and philosopher, pointed out the similarity among all members of the human race by claiming, "And so, however we may define man, a single definition will apply to all." He saw all mankind bound together by feelings of justice and by "kindliness and good-will." The Pax Romana, the Roman peace based on Roman arms, offered the blessing of peace for the great empire from which even the victims of Rome's conquests benefited. The Romans granted some privileges and rights to the conquered, subject peoples, and in A.D. 212 the Emperor Caracalla granted full citizenship to all free inhabitants of Rome, slaves excluded. This universalism was realized, however, only in appearance. Octavian, hailed as the "restorer of the commonwealth and the champion of freedom," who (to quote his own words) "handed over the republic to the control of the senate and the people of Rome," retained in sub-stance the autocratic authority he had resigned. Roman imperialism did not provide the climate in which equality could flourish.

C. The Old and New Testaments

To the Hebrews, in spite of the dissimilarities among human beings, the Lord is the maker of all men, the rich and the poor. (Prov. 22:2.) In relation to God, all men are equal and all have to fulfill His purposes and to perform His will in return for His mercy. Job, referring to his servant, asks: "Did not he that made me in the womb, make him?" (31:15.) The Psalmist proclaims that "the Lord looked from heaven; he beholdeth all the sons of men." (33:13.) Prophetic judgment is leveled at those "which oppress the poor, which crush the needy" (Amos 4:1) and those who "swallow up the needy, even to make the poor of the land to fail." (Amos 8:4.)

The prophet Amos, disturbed by the voices of those who regarded Israel as a chosen nation and as a special servant of God among the nations, cries out in the name of the Lord, "Are you not as the chil-dren of the Ethiopians unto me, O children of Israel? saith the Lord. Have not I brought up Israel out of the Land of Egypt? and the Philistines from Caphtor, and the Syrians from Kir?" (Amos 9:7.)

These attitudes are further developed in the New Testament. The idea of equality is extended by Jesus in stressing the need to serve one's fellowman.

"Whoever wants to be great must be your servant, and whoever wants to be first must be the willing slave of all." (Mark 10:43.) Although Jesus' teaching transcended all social, political, and economic circumstances, the moral discrimination between the powerful and the weak, between the rich and the poor, is maintained in the New Testament, beginning with Mary's *Magnificat:* "He has torn imperial powers from their thrones, but the humble have been lifted high. The hungry he has satisfied with good things, the rich sent empty away." Jesus' blessing upon the poor and His woes upon the rich, as recorded in the Beatitudes in Luke, maintain the same moral discrimination and concern for the weak and the oppressed.

Christianity extended the concept of equality to all. The chosen people of Israel are not the only children of God, since, as Paul explained in his letter to the Galatians, "there is no such thing as Jew and Greek, slave and freeman, male and female; for you are all one person in Christ Jesus." (3:28.) The same message of the universal nature of equality is repeated in Paul's letter to the Colossians (3:10) and by Peter, who at the invitation of the gentile Cornelius addressed a large gathering: "I now see how true it is that God has no favorites, but that in every nation the man who is godfearing and does what is right is acceptable to him." (Acts 10:34.)

D. The Feudal Society of the Middle Ages

In the Middle Ages, the feudal social organization typical of all Western Europe was based on a strict class division into three main categories, the nobility, the clergy, and the peasants. The church reflected this feudal organization and accepted its social stratification. Its hierarchy somewhat paralleled the feudal hierarchy of nobles. The church owned much land, which was held in the hands of the monasteries, the churches themselves, and the church dignitaries, who lived in splendor much like that of the powerful nobles, while some of the priests lived in base poverty. By association with the civil power, the church expanded its influence and grew rich through gifts and bequests given by pious nobles.

Although such figures as Saint Francis of Assisi carried out vows of poverty, the disruptive forces of deep inequality that were present in the feudal system also divided the church itself. As adapted to the medieval feudal society, the church, full of abuses, especially in the management of its great ecclesiastical properties, was not interested in seeking human equality nor in accepting it as one of the supreme values for which the church was established. The church used Saint Augustine's idea about God's saving grace as the first step toward salvation (later developed by Calvin and the Jansenists in their predestination theologies) to interpret and to justify worldly inequalities and sufferings.

Starting in the fourteenth century, there were movements for ecclesiastical reform, such as those launched by the Lollards and the Anabaptists. The Lollards, led by John Wycliffe (whose books were ordered burned by a papal bill in 1410), claimed that the clergy by becoming rich had abandoned the church's mission. In contrast, they spread the idea of the establishment of evangelical poverty. The Anabaptists (distinguished from the Baptists) also advocated far-reaching social and economic reforms. Their social views were determined by their belief in the equality that should reign in absolute brotherhood in Christ.

E. The Protestant Reformation

Martin Luther, the leader of the Protestant Reformation, sought to suppress the Anabaptist movement, which was one of the factors of the Peasant War of 1524–1525. Luther, who drew a sharp line between political and spiritual jurisdiction, condemned the peasants' uprising against serfdom as a revolt against civil authority. Luther's conviction that a society should have unequal classes, that "some are free, others captives, some masters, others subjects," and his distrust of merchants and peasants relate to the economic conditions of the sixteenth century. Yet, in spiritual life, Luther in a very real sense stressed equality.

Luther revolted, not against the church, but against the corruption and exploitation of the church by the Papacy, against the church as an empire. He denounced monopolies, describing those who establish them as "not worthy to be called human beings . . . for their envy and avarice are so coarse and shameless. . . ." He preached passionately against usury and extortioners. Although he accepted the existing social hierarchy with its institution of serfdom as a necessary foundation of society, he vindicated the spiritual freedom of the individual.

God, according to Luther, speaks as a voice in the heart of each individual and not through the mediation of the priesthood. He advocated that the canon law should therefore be abolished. It is intolerable, he wrote, "that in canon law so much importance is attached to the freedom, life, [and] property of the clergy. . . . If a priest is killed, the land is laid under interdict—why not when a peasant is killed? Whence comes this great distinction between those who are equally Christian?"

Calvinism differs theologically from Lutheranism chiefly in the doctrine of predestination. (To many, Calvinism is synonymous with predestination.) John Calvin, the French Protestant Reformer, insisted more than Luther on the doctrine of an eternal decree of God that out of free grace saves some people, but not others. This decision of whom to elect is predestination to salvation. Therefore, Calvin maintained that "all are not created on equal terms, but some are preordained to eternal life, others to eternal damnation." Among the "preordained" to be saved, there is no distinction of persons—all are equal in the sight of God. Calvin's idea of social reconstruction through the supervision of the church denied the existing hierarchy of offices. God's commandment to the individual to work for the divine glory, according to Calvin, calls for the avoidance of all spontaneous enjoyment of life without distinction of rank or wealth.

F. The Levellers and the Diggers

Lutheranism and Calvinism greatly influenced the

Puritan Revolution in England. In the seventeenth century the Levellers, an English politico-religious movement, aimed at religious and political equality (the term Levellers was pejorative, because of their purpose of making all men "level" to fulfill the prophecy of Isaiah 40:4). Their leader, John Lilburne (1614–1657), in his pamphlet *The Free Man's Freedom Vindicated* found "it unnatural, irrational, sinful, wicked, unjust, devilish, and tyrannical . . . for any man whatsoever, spiritual or temporal, clergyman or layman, to appropriate and assume unto himself, a power, authority, and jurisdiction, to rule, govern, or reign over any sort of men in the world without their free consent. . . ." The Levellers argued that the authority of the state should rest upon an Agreement of the People, drafted by the representatives of the rank and file in Cromwell's army. Under such an agreement, the authority of the republic should be vested in one representative house elected once each two years by full manhood suffrage.

The Levellers' concept of equality was explained by Colonel Rainborough in the Putney debate of 1647 between the officers and the soldiers of Cromwell's army:

"For really I think that the poorest he that is in England hath a life to live, as the greatest he; and therefore truly, sir, I think it's clear, that every man that is to live under a government ought first by his own consent to put himself under that government; and I do think that the poorest man in England is not at all bound in a strict sense to that government that he hath not had a voice to put himself under."

While the Levellers made a contribution to the development of the idea of political equality, a small left-wing group of the Levellers known as the Diggers stressed the interdependence of political and economic equality. Their leader, Gerrard Winstanley, in his pamphlet *The Law of Freedom in a Platform*, pointed out that economic conditions are the root of tyranny. There is no need, he wrote, for one person to be richer than another, "for Riches make men vainglorious, proud, and to oppress their Brethren; and are occasion of wars." The Diggers believed that "common land" should be distributed among the poor to cultivate.

"The State of Nature"

A. *Spinoza*

During the remainder of the seventeenth century, the idea of equality dominated the thought of prominent philosophers, such as Spinoza, Hobbes, and Locke. In his *Theologico-Political Treatise*, Spinoza stated that the best life is secured in democracy, which he defined as "a society which wields all its power as a whole." Of all forms of government he saw democracy

"as the most natural and the most consonant with individual liberty. In it no one transfers his natural right so absolutely that he has no further voice in affairs; he only hands it over to the majority of a society of which he is a unit. Thus all men remain equals, as they were in the state of nature."

Spinoza saw perils in "the state of nature," in which "everyone did everything he liked and reason's claim was lowered to a par with those of hatred and anger." To avoid these perils, Spinoza maintained, individuals by social compact hand over their natural rights to the sovereign power. The sovereign has the right to impose "any commands he pleases," and it is through the laws he enacts that justice and injustice arise.

B. Hobbes

The perils of the state of nature were also stressed by the English philosopher Thomas Hobbes, the author of *Leviathan,* one of the most prominent political treatises in European literature in the seventeenth century. According to Hobbes, men are by nature equal in bodily and mental capabilities. Because of this natural equality, men seek and pursue their own conservation and have equal hopes of attaining the ends to which they are naturally impelled. In the nature of man, stated Hobbes, we find three principal causes that lead to a state of war with one another: competition, mistrust, and a desire for glory. In this state of war, "force and fraud" are the "cardinal virtues"; the individual is dependent on his own strength for his security, and "the notions of

right and wrong, justice and injustice, have no place."
Only through the organization of society and the
establishment of a commonwealth can peace be
obtained.

C. Locke

The English philosopher John Locke, on the other
hand, saw a radical difference between the state of
nature and the state of war. He rejected completely
Hobbes's concept of the state of nature. In Locke's
view "all men are naturally in that state and remain
so till by their own consent they make themselves
members of some political society." Force, exercised
without right, constitutes a violation of the state of
nature. The proper state of nature is where people
live together "according to reason, without a common superior on earth with authority to judge
between them. . . ." For Hobbes, natural law meant
power, fraud, and force. For Locke, natural law
meant the universally accepted moral law promul-
gated by human reason as it reflects on God and on
man's relation to God. This relation calls for the
fundamental equality of all men as rational creatures
endowed with reason.

The principal new thoughts during the Enlightenment about the right to liberty and equality can be
traced to Locke and to his assertion that a man enters
this world not already equipped with ideas but with
a mind that is a *tabula rasa*, blank and ready to be
shaped by experience. According to Locke, the
natural moral law is discoverable by reason, and the
state of nature is the state of liberty. "The state of

nature," he taught, "has a law of nature to govern, which obliges every one; and reason, which is that law, teaches all mankind ... that, being all equal and independent, no one ought to harm another in his life, health, liberty, or possessions." Thus Locke's theory of intellectual development implied the rejection of the basis of traditional hereditary inequalities.

Men, stated Locke, were endowed with certain natural rights even before there was a state. He based his exposition of individual liberty and equality on natural law and on his idea of a social contract arrived at by people in building their society. This social contract theory argues that sovereignty resides in the people, who have the moral right to overthrow a government that does not reflect the popular will.

D. Rousseau

The state of nature was also widely discussed by Jean Jacques Rousseau, the most frequently quoted thinker of eighteenth-century France. He has been praised as a prominent philosopher and ridiculed as an eccentric; he has been studied seriously as an influential theorist of his time and rebuffed for his lack of historical perspective and for deficiencies in his knowledge of history. His first major publication, the *Discourse on the Arts and Sciences*, which made him suddenly famous, was written in response to a contest offered by the Academy of Dijon for the best answer to the question, "Has the progress of the arts and sciences tended to the purification or the corruption of morality?" In the prize-winning essay, published in 1750, Rousseau gave a defiantly negative answer. As a popularizer of the idea of the "noble savage," he distrusted the idea of progress.

The myth of a natural man uncorrupted by the advances of civilization was so enticing to Rousseau that he could see only corruption in the advent of new development in the arts and sciences. In the second part of the *Discourse*, he stated, "Astronomy was born from superstition, eloquence from ambition, hate, flattery and falsehood; geometry from avarice; physics from vain curiosity; all, even moral philosophy, from human pride. Thus the sciences and arts owe their birth to our vices." (Translated by Roger D. and Judith R. Masters, St. Martin's Press, 1964, p. 48.)

Rousseau tried to support this thesis by references to history. When the Goths ravaged Greece, he wrote, they saved the libraries from burning in order to turn the enemies away from military exercise "and amuse them with idle and sedentary occupations." The military virtue of Romans died, he argued, when they "became connoisseurs of paintings, engravings, [and] jeweled vessels, and began to cultivate the fine arts." The most evident effect and the most dangerous consequence of the arts and sciences, concluded Rousseau, is "the disastrous inequality introduced among men by the destruction of talents and the debasement of virtues."

Five years later the Academy of Dijon also offered a prize for the best essay on the question, "What is the origin of inequality among men and is it in accordance with the natural law?" Rousseau's *Discourse on the Origin and Foundations of Inequality Among Men* did not win the prize, but it was published in 1758.

The greatest social interest of men in a society is, according to this *Discourse*, the inhibition of inequality. The worst of all social evils is thus institutional inequality. Rousseau argued that man living outside society was "wandering up and down the forests without industry, without speech and without home, an equal stranger to war and to all ties, neither standing in need of his fellow-creatures nor having any desire to hurt them." His fundamental impulse was self-love in the sense of the impulse of self-preservation. When he took note of his fellows, a second impulse of compassion came into operation.

In the pure state of nature all men had been equal. When they found their existence threatened by violence and war, they concluded a social contract that led to a political community that would judge conflicts between individuals and regulate "the choice and power of magistrates" charged with enforcement of law and order. It also led to the transformation of mere possession into a lawful right to property in which Rousseau saw the cause "of crimes, wars, murders, miseries, and horrors."

The idea of the equality of the natural man undergirds Rousseau's theory of the General Will. It may be mentioned that he did not invent the phrase "general will," but he determined its history. It was Montesquieu who saw in legislative power the "general will *(volunté general)* of the state," while the role of the executive power was the execution of the general will. Unlike Montesquieu, Rousseau refused to accept the sort of civil liberty that existed only among the aristocrats in the Europe of his day. It is wrong, he wrote, that "the privileged few should gorge themselves with superfluities while the starving multitude is in want of the base necessities of life."

Rousseau, at one time closely associated with Denis Diderot, also rejected Diderot's notion of the general will as the universal bond obliging mankind. The belief in progress and enlightenment, emphasized in Diderot's *Encyclopedia*, was challenged by Rousseau in his aforementioned view that the arts and sciences have a corrupting influence on equality and are unrelated to true virtue. The general will, argued Rousseau, is the voice of the people, in fact the voice of God *(vox populi, vox dei)*. The important role of a legitimate and popular government is "to follow in everything the general will," and the "first duty of the legislator is to make the laws conformable to the general will."

Rousseau's state of nature was, not the state of "war of all against all" *(homo homini lupus)* that Hobbes described, but a state of egalitarian independence. Like a peaceful animal, primitive man was "satisfying his hunger at the first oak and slaking his thirst at the first brook, finding his bed at the foot of the tree which afforded him a repast; and with that, all his wants [were] supplied." The rise of moral and political inequality, according to Rousseau, should be attributed to the establishment of private property, to the improvement of human faculties, and to the establishment of political society, government, and law. In his account of the origin of inequality, Rousseau saw three stages: The first stage was the establishment of the law and of the right of property, the second was the institution of government, and the third and last "was the changing of legitimate power into arbitrary power."

Rousseau was right in describing tyrannical rule as "the last stage of inequality." A full circle takes place when we arrive at despotism. Men return to their first equality when the tyrant reduces them to slaves. Then inequality becomes the equality of slaves. All Rousseau's other conclusions, however, can hardly be applied to modern society. His ideal political system was that of a small city-state in which the body of patriotic citizens is sovereign and the citizens in a straightforward, democratic manner vote in a popular assembly. In large states such assemblies are impracticable.

Furthermore, the *First Discourse* and the *Second Discourse* are full of contradictions and paradoxes. Rousseau loathed scholars and intellectuals generally, yet he wrote his discourses for the learned Academy of Dijon. He himself acknowledged this contradiction by asking, "How can one dare blame the sciences before one of Europe's most learned societies, praise ignorance in a famous Academy, and reconcile contempt for study with respect for the truly learned?" Many of his other writings also have a paradoxical character. In the book *Emile*, Rousseau admitted, "Common readers, pardon my paradoxes; they must be made when one thinks seriously; and, whatever you may say, I would rather be a man of paradoxes than a man of prejudices." But the reduction of the natural man to a peaceful but unthinking animal is not a matter of prejudices. It is a paradox of such a pernicious sort that it prompted Voltaire to call the *Discourse on Inequality* a "book against the human race."

Equality as a Vehicle of Vindictiveness

As discussed above, the view of human equality emphasized in the Old and New Testaments—as well as the view of many subsequent religious leaders and philosophers—concentrated on the arrogance of the rich and powerful and the humility of the poor. But do the poor and humble retain their humility when they cease to be poor and themselves become the wielders of power? The passion for equality can turn into a vehicle of vindictiveness when those who seek equality, upon gaining power, exhibit the same arrogance and cruelty that they abhorred in their oppressors. The French and Bolshevik revolutions give vivid illustrations of what happens when the fortunes of events transmute the weakness of the oppressed into strength and desire for power.

A. The French Revolution

In France at the end of the eighteenth century, the tension caused by the deep-seated discontent of the unprivileged lower classes became intolerable. The privileges of the nobles and of the clergy became onerous burdens on the peasants, the working classes, and the bourgeoisie. The middle class, or bourgeoisie, built up by the expansion of commerce and the growing popularity of the laissez-faire doctrine of Adam Smith, clamored for power. Three estates formed the legislative body: The First Estate consisted of the upper clergy; the Second Estate, of nobles; and the Third Estate, of the lower clergy, the

bourgeoisie, and artisans. This theoretical representation did little for the lower orders, however. The
heavily taxed lower classes could not exert any power,
because the king refused to convoke the legislature.

The Paris mob, discontented because of the
prevailing misrule, disorder, corruption, and financial chaos, revolted and on July 14, 1789, stormed and
destroyed the prison of the Bastille. The insurrection
spread rapidly throughout France. Chateaus belong-
ing to nobility were burned, the owners murdered
or driven away, tax collectors assaulted. Headed by
Jean Paul Marat, the radical Commune of Paris,
which replaced the Paris government, and the radical Jacobins, with Robespierre as their leader, were
blinded by the extreme idea of "liberty and equality" and were responsible for the September Mas-
sacres of 1792, when thousands of aristocrats, priests,
and others suspected of hostility to the revolution
were murdered.

During the same month, the monarchy was
abolished and the First Republic established. Louis
XVI, convicted of treason, was guillotined in January of 1793. The Revolutionary Tribunal went to
work, and the Reign of Terror began. Opulence was
proclaimed "infamous." To obtain equality, the
rulers taxed property and confiscated it to be divided
among the poor. The guillotine became the official
instrument of execution, and it chopped off heads
day after day, week after week. The struggle for
power among various groups resulted in an incredible butchery. The victims of the mass slaughtering
included Marat and Georges Jacques Danton, leaving

Robespierre the master of the revolution until he himself was executed on 9 Thermidor (July 27, 1794). The Great Terror brought the Thermidorian reaction. France, weary of blood, stress, and confusion, was ready to abandon the extreme of revolution. After a series of insurrections, stalemates, and coups d'etat, "New France" was ready to take on some likeness of the old, to accept Napoleon as its ruler, and to endure an emperor.

B. The Bolshevik Revolution

A parallel process to that of the rise of terror during the first French Revolution took place in Russia early in this century. The disintegration of the autocratic government of the Romanov dynasty led to the abdication of Nicholas II on March 15, 1917. The disorganization of the country that had followed the defeats suffered during World War I was extreme. With the army in a state of mutiny, the slogans of equality, liberty, and unity offered by the Bolsheviks were very appealing to the hundreds of thousands of soldiers wandering back from the war zone to their homes. The Bolsheviks' well-established tradition of terrorism and opportunism encouraged the peasants and the workers to satisfy their demands by direct action. They rose against the landowners, burned chateaus, looted houses, and robbed and murdered innocent men and women.

The election on November 17, 1917, of a Constituent Assembly produced only a 24 percent vote for the Bolsheviks. The Bolshevik-led troops, having arrested a number of the elected delegates, surrounded Petrograd's Tauride Palace, in which the Constituent Assembly met; dissolved the assembly; and moved on to establish throughout the country a one-party dictatorship. The Politburo, composed of seven members, became the governing body of the party and of Russia as well.

The changes in economic life introduced by the communists during the first three years of their regime were no less revolutionary than the changes made in Russia's political system. The results of the implementation of the fundamental concept of their economic thought—equality and justice to be obtained through preventing the capitalists and the landlords from exploiting the workers and the peasants—remind us of the observation made by the early-twentieth-century philosopher Ortega y Gasset, who said, "The mob goes in search of bread, and the means it employs is generally to wreck bakeries."

The economic system envisaged by the communist leaders called for the nationalization of all means of production, transportation, trade, and banking and of all land, forests, and minerals. In the process of the punitive nationalization of all kinds of industries, the responsibility of management was vested in workers who were not prepared by education or training. The resulting failure to coordinate the supply of raw materials, transportation, and distribution caused chaos and a collapse of industry that proved to be disastrous to Russia's economic life.

In the realm of agriculture the Soviet government seized grain by force when the peasants resorted to passive resistance against the food dictatorship established in May 1918. The peasants, who were bearing the principal burden of the cost of industrialization, had to turn over to the state all grain above the minimum needed for consumption by their families and for seed. The peasants resisted vigorously the establishment of a state monopoly in grain, and a great deal of bloodshed occurred. As a result of the reduced food supply and of the severe famine, many died from starvation.

Having antagonized the great body of the proletariat and of the peasants, the communists were forced to make concessions and to retreat by inaugurating a New Economic Policy (NEP). The NEP permitted peasants to rent land for limited periods of time and allowed small factories and shops to employ a certain number of wage laborers. A fixed tax was substituted for the system of requisitioning grain from the peasants, who were allowed to retain and dispose of freely in the open market whatever they produced over and above the amount of the imposed tax. Establishments engaged in small industry and domestic trade were restored to private enterprise. The NEP inaugurated a period of economic convalescence at a considerable sacrifice of socialist principles. The compromises made by the communists were, however, of only a temporary nature. The substance of Karl Marx's program was the nationalization of the means of production, and that program was still at the heart of Soviet intentions.

With the adoption of the 1928 Five-Year Plan, the concessions to private initiative were annulled or severely restricted. The communist party was also undergoing a great upheaval, reflecting the bitter conflict that had been going on within its own ranks.

As in the French Revolution, the leader who gained all the power rid himself of his rivals by a recourse to treason trials. Of the seven members of the 1920 Politburo, six were purged by Joseph Stalin. Following the great purge trials of 1935–1938, with their sensational confessions, those who were opposed to the Stalin regime or who voiced their discontent were liquidated by firing squad.

In agriculture the collectivization of holdings of the prosperous peasants, called kulaks, proceeded for the sake of "equality." Their houses, livestock, and tools were confiscated, and they were banished to remote concentration camps where they were compelled to furnish unpaid labor without being provided even the minimum goods needed to survive.

The Soviet secret police (the NKVD, presently the KGB) became the largest employer of labor in the nation. In the concentration camps scattered all over the country, the kulaks were joined by political opponents, members of minority groups, and others sentenced to hard labor for often-imaginary offenses. In the nation's economic planning, the secret police were responsible for carrying out a considerable segment of the capital construction planned. One of the purposes of mass arrests was thus to supply forced unpaid labor. The work to be done by forced labor included mining, producing timber, and building railroads, canals, tunnels, highways, and military camps. It was estimated that by 1940, during Stalin's time, the number of prisoners rose to perhaps as many as 20 million.

The passion for equality, as we mentioned, can

turn into a vehicle of brutality for brutality's sake. Robespierre, guided by a consuming passion for a new order of life, saw himself surrounded by wicked men, whom, in defense of humanity, he had sent to the guillotine. Stalin's repression was designed to instill fear—it often bore no relevance to the stated purposes of the communist state, which included the objective of equality. He destroyed and killed out of vindictiveness, meanness, and paranoia.

The Dangers in the Passion for Equality

The experience of the French Revolution undoubtedly prompted Alexis de Tocqueville to observe the dangers that occur when the passions engendered by the idea of equality turn violent:

"Democratic peoples always like equality, but there are times when their passion for it turns to delirium. This happens when the old social hierarchy, long menaced, finally collapses after a severe internal struggle and the barriers of rank are at length thrown down. At such times men pounce on equality as their booty and cling to it as a precious treasure they fear to have snatched away. The passion for equality seeps into every corner of the human heart, expands, and fills the whole. It is no use telling them that by this blind surrender to an exclusive passion they are compromising their dearest interests; they are deaf. It is no use pointing out that freedom is slipping from their grasp while they look the other way; they are blind, or rather they can see but one thing to covet in the whole world." (*Democracy in America*, a new translation by George Lawrence, 1966, Harper & Row, p. 475.)

It may be noted that Tocqueville thought of calling the second volume of his book *L'Egalité en Amerique* but changed the word "equality" to "democracy." Perhaps the reason for this decision was the experience of the French Revolution, which demonstrated that equality is not always a manifestation of freedom, or perhaps it was that the term "democracy" used by the Americans in President Andrew Jackson's day, when Tocqueville visited the United States, was more entrenched there and elsewhere. Tocqueville uses the term "democracy" to refer to the United States in the broadest terms. It includes the equality proclaimed in the very beginning of American history as the leading feature of the country. The unfailing faith of the American settlers that equality of conditions signifies freedom from being ruled and from ruling others prompted Tocqueville to write in his Introduction:

"No novelty in the United States struck me more vividly during my stay there than the equality of conditions. It was easy to see the immense influence of this basic fact on the whole course of society. It gives a particular turn to public opinion and a particular twist to the laws, new maxims to those who govern and particular habits to the governed.
    "I soon realized that the influence of this fact extends far beyond political government; it

creates opinions, gives birth to feelings, suggests customs, and modifies whatever it does not create.

"So the more I studied American society, the more clearly I saw equality of conditions as the creative element from which each particular fact derived, and all my observations constantly returned to this nodal point." (*Ibid.*, p. 3.)

It is noteworthy that Tocqueville repeatedly stressed that in the contest for freedom and equality, people want both, but if they cannot have freedom, "they still want equality in slavery." (*Ibid.*, p. 475.) In Chapter 1 of Volume II, Part II, of *Democracy in America*, which he entitled "Why Democratic Nations Show a More Ardent and Enduring Love for Equality than for Liberty," he explained that equality, not freedom, is the chief and continued object of mankind's desires. People, he wrote, seek freedom with "quick and sudden impulses," but if they fail to obtain it, "they resign themselves to their disappointment; but nothing will satisfy them without equality, and they would rather die than lose it." (*Ibid.*, p. 49.)

In the light of Tocqueville's observations that his contemporaries loved equality more tenaciously than liberty, how can we explain his classical account of American equality in freedom, quoted above, which implies that there is an organic relationship between equality and freedom, rather than a contest between them? How did the "equality of conditions" in the United States differ from the political experiences of other nations? What was the distinctive character of the new environment at the beginning of American history in which equality in freedom was expected to flourish.

Equality in Freedom

We can find one of the answers to these questions in the fact that the United States was the only nation aware, before it came into existence, of the purpose of equality in freedom. In other nations, in Tocqueville's time, revolutions for the sake of equality erupted as a reaction against corruption, abuse, brutality, and exploitation. When the revolution succeeded in overthrowing the ruling government, the masters of the revolution took the place of the oppressors. A mass of citizens confused about their rights and duties fell easily under the yoke of new rulers, who often proved to be more barbaric than the governments that collapsed.

The settlers of the United States did not come here to establish political dominion over others. They came, not to rehabilitate an ancient organization of society by giving it an improved form, but to start a new nation with a new purpose—a project which had never been tried before. This new historic process started long before the American Revolution. As John Adams wrote to a Dr. Mise on January 1, 1816, the war for independence was "not a revolutionary war, for the revolution was complete, in the minds of the people, and the union of the colonies, before the war commenced in the skirmishes of Concord and Lexington on the 19th of April 1775."

The Pilgrims of the *Mayflower* left an old society behind them, and they had no intention of accepting its principles as a pattern for the new society they were determined to build. The society they founded had a radically different purpose from those of existing societies. This purpose was equality in freedom—a freedom that offered each man the opportunity to rise as high as merit would carry him. This was the reason for our nation's existence as an independent entity. The Founding Fathers, in the Declaration of Independence, set forth this purpose of personal equality in freedom as a fundamental tenet of this nation's political faith.

Equality of Opportunity—Economic Equality

We can find another answer to the questions posed above in the distinctive American concept of equality, which differed dramatically from the deeply rooted tradition of social hierarchy in Europe, where a person's principal distinguishing quality was his birth and where the rich and the poor were far removed from each other socially as well as economically. The American ideal of equality focused on the opportunity for each citizen to make his own place in the society, with none excluded by birth from access to political rule. Describing contemporary society in the United States in his *Letters from an American Farmer*, the American author J. Hector St. John (1735–1813) wrote:

> "It is not composed, as in Europe, of great lords who possess everything, and of herds of people who have nothing. There are no aristocratical families, no courts, no kings, no bishops, no ecclesiastical dominion, no invisible power giving

to a few a very visible one; no great manufacturers employing thousands, no great refinement of luxury. . . . We have no princes for whom we toil, starve and bleed; we are the most perfect society now existing in the world. Here man is free as he ought to be; nor is this pleasing equality so transitory as many others are."

In the same spirit, Benjamin Franklin, the statesman and scientist who was the first American to become widely known abroad, advised those "who would remove to America" about the new American society: "There are few great proprietors of the soil, and few tenants; most people cultivate their own lands, or follow some handicraft or merchandise; very few [are] rich enough to live idly upon their rents or incomes. . . ." The would-be immigrants to America, he wrote, should therefore expect a different world from the one they lived in in Europe, since they would find in the United States "few people so miserable as the poor of Europe" and also "very few that in Europe would be called rich[;] it is rather a general happy mediocrity that prevails."

It should also be noted that the American concept of equality in freedom differed in substance from the equality espoused by the French Revolution or the Marxists. The European egalitarianism advocated that all men should occupy a uniform position on a common level in wealth, income, and power. The American idea of equality stressed equality in opportunity, which can lift men from rags to riches, from the log cabin to the White House, and put strong emphasis upon freedom as the means to make equality a reality. It asserted unalienable birthrights of everybody in all areas of life. Individual status depended not upon inherited but upon achieved qualities. Benjamin Franklin expressed this explicitly when he said that in America people "do not inquire concerning a stranger: *What is he?* but *What can he do?*"

American equality did not demand equality of wealth and income or advocate the confiscation of property and its division among the poor and homeless. Abraham Lincoln advised, "Let not him who is houseless pull down the house of another, but let him work diligently and build one for himself, thus by example assuring that his home should be safe from violence when built."

To answer the question of what the distinctive character of the environment at the beginning of American history was that gave hopes for equality in freedom to flourish, we find the Charter of James I of 1620, which says:

> "[T]he appointed time is come in which Almighty God in his great goodness and bounty . . . has thought fit and determined, that those large and goodly territories, deserted as it were by their natural inhabitants, should be possessed and enjoyed by such of our subjects and people as heretofore have and hereafter shall by his mercy and favor. . . ."

Four million people, poor but with the potentiality of acquiring limitless wealth, were scattered over a vast area. The settlers, rich in land and released from the institutions that had evolved in Europe in the past, planned the United States as a country where the idea of equality in freedom would stand out very prominently. This idea could be realized only in the kind of environment described by John Adams:

> "In the present state of society and manners in America, with a people living chiefly by agriculture, in small numbers, sprinkled over large tracts of land, they are not subject to those panics and transports, those contagions of madness and folly, which are seen in countries where large numbers live in small places, in daily fear of perishing for want. We know, therefore, that the people can live and increase under almost any kind of government, or without any government at all."

The early settler, compared by John Locke to a "king of a large and fruitful territory" but "clad worse than a day-labourer in England," sought a political equality that would provide him an effective share in the policy decisions that would shape the life of the community in which he lived. The empty spaces of fertile land meant that he had, not only equality of opportunity to provide for his material needs and to secure the good things of life, but the conditions in which the opportunity could exist. In the vast territories he did not find the social barriers and the irrational social discrimination of the "old society." His right to belong to associations of his choice and to participate in group life, although "sprinkled over large tracts of land," provided him with civil and legal equality.

"The Great American Experiment"

The faith of the founders of the United States that the Creator has endowed all human beings with the right to be free and to have equal opportunity endowed our nation with a sense of mission that was expressed in the opening paragraph of *The Federalist* papers. By our "conduct and example," it was said, our people hoped to demonstrate to all the world the advantage of a free and self-governing society. This mission became known as the "great American experiment."

The equalization of opportunity in political, economic, religious, and social life became known as the "American dream." The hope that this great American experiment would serve as an example for other nations to emulate was also expressed by Abraham Lincoln, who asserted that the Declaration of Independence gave "liberty, not alone to the people of this country, but hope to the world for all future time." It gave "promise that in due time the weights should be lifted from the shoulders of all men. . . ." All the world looked on to see whether the American dream would materialize.

This dream, however, has never been fully realized. There was a serious gap between the ideals and the practices of the American republic. What was the cause of this gap? We may also ask why the dream never ceased to inspire this nation to raise its voice on behalf of equal opportunities for jobs, homes, education, and good health. Why does the United States remain the only hope of the oppressed everywhere? What is the magnetic power this country has to attract men and women of all races and religions, all colors and creeds, to come here to escape tyranny and discrimination?

Slavery and the "Three Compromises"

To answer these questions, we should start with the admission that throughout our history there have been flagrant violations utterly contrary to the idea of equality in freedom. Slavery was one of the most significant obstacles standing in the way of the fulfillment of the American dream. Slavery, having begun with the enslavement of Indians for work in plantations and mines, had been an American institution for over a century and a half before the War of Independence. Historians tell us that 1620, when the Pilgrim Fathers landed in Plymouth in New England, was also the year when a Dutch sloop disembarked the first cargo of Negroes at Jamestown in Virginia. The Negroes toiled under the whip of the overseer when Thomas Jefferson penned the Declaration of Independence, which spoke of self-evident truths, the foremost of which was that each and every individual is endowed by our Creator with "certain unalienable rights—and that among them are Life, Liberty, and the Pursuit of Happiness."

In 1795, Thomas Paine wrote in the "Dissertation on First Principles" that "the principle of equality of rights is clear and simple. Every man can understand it, and it is by understanding his rights that he learns his duties; for where the rights of man are equal, every man finally sees the necessity of protecting the rights of others as the most effectual security of his own." But this principle was not quite "simple" since it did not include blacks, native Americans, or women. Hardly could "every man" be said to understand this principle since the provisions of the unamended Constitution written in 1787 included the famous "three compromises" that have been called the source of the Civil War fought three-quarters of a century later.

The word "slavery" does not appear in the Constitution until we reach the Thirteenth Amendment, adopted after the Civil War. Such circumlocutions as a "person held to service or labor" or "such persons as any of the States now existing shall think proper to admit" are used to avoid the word "slave." The first of the three compromises we find in the famous "three-fifths" clause, Clause 3 of Article I, Section 2. It refers to the apportionment of taxes among the states, "according to their respective Numbers, which shall be determined by adding to the whole number of free persons, including those bound to service for a term of years, and excluding Indians not taxed, three-fifths of all other persons."

Thus three-fifths of the slaves were counted in laying taxes and in ascertaining how many members a state should have in the House of Representatives. The northern states claimed that slave-holding states would be undertaxed by not counting the slaves as population. The South claimed that those states would be overtaxed by counting the slaves. Furthermore, since the number of representatives from any state would be apportioned according to its population, slave-state delegates to the Constitutional Convention favored including every slave, although the slaves were not citizens or voters and had no influence on the lawmaking process. Delegates from the nonslave northern states were opposed to counting slaves. The compromise of equating five black men for three white men that was made for the purposes of taxation was also used to determine representation in the House. By combining the two opposed purposes, direct taxation and representation, a restraint was established that prevented a state from getting too much representation and avoiding the payment of its share of direct taxes.

The second compromise, which we find in Section 9 of Article I, postponed abolition of the slave trade for twenty years (until 1808). The third compromise respecting slavery, found in Section 2 of Article IV, was designed to assure the slave-holding states that slaves who might flee to northern states would not become free. (In 1772, Lord Mansfield, Chief Justice of the King's Bench, declared in the celebrated case of a black man named Somerset that a slave brought by his master from Virginia to England became free.)

The three compromises, and especially the three-fifths clause, may explain the position of the U. S. Supreme Court in the case of *Dred Scott v. John F. A. Stanford* (19 How. 393–638, 15 L. Ed. 691 [1857]), in which Chief Justice Taney declared that Negroes were a subordinate and "inferior class" of beings and ascribed to the founders of the Constitution the intention to perpetuate the "impassable barrier" between the white race and the whole "enslaved African race" (including mulattoes). The Court further concluded that Negroes are "altogether unfit to associate with the white race, either in social or political relations and so far inferior, that they had no rights which the white man was bound to respect. . . ." (*Ibid.*, p. 407.)

Because of the three compromises, especially the three-fifths clause, some citizens denounced the celebration of the bicentennial honoring the Constitution in 1987. They refused to celebrate a historical document that permitted slavery to continue and that expressed the view that a black is only a fraction of a human being. It may be argued that in the struggle between proslavery and antislavery forces the compromises offered the only chance of a union that would include the South. It may also be argued that Chief Justice Taney was wrong since at the Constitutional Convention the Founders stressed that the principles of the Declaration of Independence would remain the bedrock foundation of the Constitution and, in order to save the union, accepted the continuation of slavery as an unavoidable evil. These arguments would not change the fact that compromises that degrade moral values, the human spirit, and human dignity cannot survive or calm down the voices demanding an end to brutality and exploitation. The so-called compromises did not prevent the bloody Civil War, which was followed by constitutional amendments that expanded our definition of equality to encompass minorities and women.

Setbacks to the Commitment

Even with this expanded definition, our country has not had an unblemished record. Setbacks and controversies arose from actual denial of the moral commitment of the Founding Fathers, who dedicated this country to the purpose of freedom for all. America did not remain faithful to their commitment, nor to the legal commitment of the Constitution. The list of disappointments is too long to deal with other than in the broadest way, and we will merely mention some examples that became a part of the American experience of denial of the American purpose. Among the crippling blows, besides the above-mentioned *Dred Scott* decision that foreshadowed the crisis of the Civil War, was the 1896 U. S. Supreme Court decision *Plessy v. Ferguson,* where the Court adopted the doctrine of "separate but equal" by taking the position that the object of the Fourteenth Amendment was not to abolish distinctions based upon color or to enforce social, as distinguished from political, equality, "or commingling of two races upon terms unsatisfactory to either." The Court suggested that legislatures were powerless to eradicate racial instincts, and "if one race is inferior to the other socially, the Constitution of the United States cannot put them upon the same plane."

The separation of the two races resulted in the establishment of separate schools for each and of separate theaters, hotels, restaurants, and railway carriages. The separate-but-equal doctrine spread to parks, playgrounds, swimming pools, and beaches. Because they were barred from the ballot box, blacks had no political influence to remedy these situations. This doctrine lasted 58 years, until the historical unanimous ruling of the U. S. Supreme Court of May 17, 1954, in *Brown v. Board of Education of Topeka, Kansas.*

As we have seen, there were deplorable departures from the concept of equality and freedom, but it should be pointed out that whenever there was a blundering reversion to inequality (and there were many of them) the voice of conscience could still be heard calling for adherence to the ideal of equal access to "life, liberty, and the pursuit of happiness." There were shortcomings in the implementation of equality in freedom, but the strong thread of moral purpose that runs through the fabric of American history should never be ignored or underestimated.

As early as 1769, Thomas Jefferson had urged the Assembly in Virginia to emancipate the slaves in the colony. One of Jefferson's accusations against the crown of Great Britain was that any attempt by the colonists to restrain the slave trade had been checked by the greedy proprietary interest of slave traders in the mother country. (The slave traffic, in the words of Lord Darmouth, was "so beneficient to the nation" that the colonies should not be allowed to check or discourage it.)

Thomas Paine, a few weeks after coming to America, in an essay published March 8, 1775, denounced slavery as no less immoral than "murder, robbery, lewdness, and barbarity." Deploring the "wicked and inhuman ways" used by the slave traders—"the desperate wretches" who "enslave men by violence and murder for gain"—he declared, "So much innocent blood have the managers and supporters of this inhuman trade to answer for to the common Lord of all!"

President Lincoln, reacting to the *Dred Scott* decision, argued that "it is not factious, it is even not disrespectful, to treat it as not having yet quite established a settled doctrine for the Country." Since this decision had not been made by the unanimous concurrence of the Justices and had not been affirmed and reaffirmed through a course of years, he stated, it would not be "revolutionary, to not acquiesce in it as a precedent."

Because of the experience of the Civil War, restrictions that would have been impossible before the war were imposed on the states. To remove the legal doubts about the validity of the Emancipation Proclamation (since it was made under the President's war power) and to liberate slaves everywhere in the country, the Thirteenth Amendment was adopted. It provides that neither slavery nor involuntary servitude shall exist within the United States or any place subject to its jurisdiction. In practice the Thirteenth Amendment was found to be insufficient. The Supreme Court pointed out that in some states the former slaves continued to be forbidden to appear in towns other than as menial servants, that they did not have the right to purchase or own land, that they were not permitted to give testimony in the courts in any case where a white man was a party, and that they were subject to numerous discriminations.

The Equal Protection Clause of the Fourteenth Amendment, adopted July 21, 1868, was primarily written for the liberated blacks, although they are not mentioned in the amendment. The clause was designed to prevent a state from making discriminations between its own citizens because of race,

color, or "previous conditions of servitude." (See also
the Fifteenth Amendment.) Chief Justice William
Howard Taft made a distinction between due process
and equal protection when he explained that "the
spheres of the protection they offer are not coter-
minous." Due process, he stated, offers a minimum
protection, while equal protection offers a supplemental guarantee. As a supplemental guarantee,
the Equal Protection Clause has its own reason for
existence and should not be regarded as an incidental right attached to the Due Process Clause. (*Truax
v. Corrigan*, 257 U. S. 312, 332, 42 S. Ct. 124, 129
[1921].)

The Voice of National Conscience

The thread of moral purpose, which had always
existed but was not always highly visible, came to the
surface when Justice John Marshall Harlan in his lone
dissent in the case of *Plessy v. Ferguson* wrote:

> "The white race deems itself to be the dominant
> race in this country, and so it is. . . . But in view
> of the Constitution, in the eye of the law, there
> is in this country no superior, dominant ruling
> class of citizen. There is no class here. Our Con-
> stitution is color blind. In respect to civil rights
> all citizens are equal before the law."

In this century the voice of national conscience
became louder. It was heard when President Harry
Truman presented to the Congress his 1948 Message
on Civil Rights, in which he recommended estab-

lishing a permanent Commission on Civil Rights, a
Joint Congressional Committee on Civil Rights, and
a Civil Rights Division in the Department of Justice;
strengthening protection against lynching; providing
more adequate protection for the right to vote; establishing a Fair Employment Practice Commission
to prevent unfair discrimination in employment; prohibiting discrimination in interstate transportation
facilities; and equalizing the opportunities for residents of the United States to become naturalized
citizens.

It was President Lyndon B. Johnson who, referring
to the Civil Rights Act of 1964, stated:

> "The denial of rights invites increased disorder
> and violence, and those who would hold back
> progress toward equality, and at the same time
> promise racial peace, are deluding themselves
> and deluding the people. Orderly progress, exact
> enforcement of law are the only paths to end
> racial strife."

The Emancipation, declared President Johnson, was
a proclamation, not a fact. The compassionate and
comprehensive civil rights legislation that passed
with the votes of more than two-thirds of the members of both parties of the Congress was a fact, since
the laws rightly passed must be observed. (Address
delivered before the American Bar Association, New
York, N. Y., August 12, 1964.) And again, advocating the Voting Rights Act at Howard University on
June 4, 1965, President Johnson called for equality
not just "as right and theory but equality as a fact
and equality as a result."

Senator Hubert Humphrey, discussing the purpose of Title VI of the Civil Rights Act of 1964, said:

"The bill has a simple purpose. That purpose is to give fellow citizens—Negroes—the same rights and opportunities that white people take for granted. This is no more than what was preached by the prophets, and by Christ Himself. It is no more than what our Constitution guarantees." (110 Cong. Rec. 655 [1964].)

Discrimination Against Women

The purpose of Title VI of the Civil Rights Act is not limited to giving equal rights to Negroes. Through the years women also had not had legal protection against discrimination. English common law did not regard women as legal persons or entities. Since the U. S. Constitution was adopted under the influence of English common law, the decisions of the Supreme Court as late as 1961 did not declare unconstitutional the laws of some states that limited the rights of married women. The discrimination against women consisted in limiting their right to make contracts, have separate domiciles, dispose of property by will, engage in business, exercise the guardianship of children, and participate fully in other important fields of American life.

Women are not mentioned in the Constitution, nor do the words "man," "male," or any other noun or adjective denoting sex occur in the original document. (The Northwest Ordinance, adopted the same year as the Constitution, gave the right to vote and to representation in the general assembly only to "free male inhabitants.") The pronouns used by the Constitution—"he," "himself," and "his"—are as genderless as the nouns "mankind" or, until recently, "chairman." The Fifth Amendment provides that no person shall be compelled in any criminal case to be a witness against himself. There was never any doubt whatsoever that the protection offered by this amendment extends also to women. Although under the Constitution women had equal rights with men, in practice they did not enjoy political equality. The early, largely agricultural American community disregarded women as citizens.

Because the Fourteenth Amendment does not mention women, in the absence of a special guarantee of their rights, the fight for their emancipation continued to grow under the leadership of such courageous reformers as Lucy Stone (1818–1893), Susan Brownell Anthony (1820–1906), Elizabeth Cady Stanton (1815–1902), and others who struggled through all available means to promote the women's suffrage movement. Lucy Stone in 1870 founded the *Woman's Journal,* which was for nearly 50 years the official organ of the National American Suffrage Association. Susan B. Anthony and Elizabeth Stanton secured the first laws in New York guaranteeing women's rights over their children, control of property and wages, and a separate legal existence after marriage. The battle for women's suffrage was won in the United States in 1920 (20 years earlier than in France, 2 years later than in Great Britain and Germany). The Nineteenth Amendment, proclaimed August 20, 1920, rendered ineffective the provisions in many acts of Congress and in many state constitutions that had deprived women of suffrage before this amendment. The fight for equal rights for women has continued throughout the twentieth century.

Civil Rights Legislation

Because the voice of conscience demonstrated that important changes in social values and concerns had occurred, the Equal Protection Clause of the Fourteenth Amendment needed implementation to broaden the scope of protection against discrimination based on race, sex, age, creed, and physical handicap. Executive orders issued by our Presidents to curtail such discrimination lacked adequate means of enforcement. (The first such order was issued by President Franklin D. Roosevelt to create the Fair Employment Practices Commission.) The civil rights legislation of the last two decades—to mention only the Civil Rights Act of 1964 and the Voting Rights Act of 1965, numerous federal regulations and state laws designed to eliminate discrimination, and the current array of legal measures to promote equal employment opportunity—offers more effective and farther-reaching remedies against the barriers of discrimination than does the Equal Protection Clause of the Fourteenth Amendment.

The interpretation of the civil rights legislation by the Supreme Court has established the constitutionality of race-conscious remedial measures. The Court has construed Title VII of the Civil Rights Act of 1964

as requiring the use of racial preferences for the purpose of hiring and advancing those who have been
adversely affected by past discriminatory employment practices, even at the expense of other
employees innocent of discrimination. Federal regulations also clearly establish that race-conscious action is not only permitted but required to accomplish
the remedial objectives of Title VII. The choice of
remedies to redress racial discrimination is "a balancing process left, within appropriate constitutional or
statutory limits, to the sound discretion of the trial
court." (*Franks v. Bowman Transportation Co.*, 424 U.
S. 747, 96 S. Ct. [1976].)

The Supreme Court, in a 1987 opinion delivered
by Justice William Brennan, took the position that
the manifest imbalance reflecting underrepresentation of women and minorities in traditionally
segregated jobs allows the employer to adopt an affirmative action plan and take sex or race into
account without violating Title VII. For the purpose
of remedying such underrepresentation, the employer, stated the Court, did not "trammel the rights of
male employees" by promoting a woman over a male
employee with a higher test score.

In order to determine whether there is an imbalance reflecting underrepresentation of women
and minorities in traditionally segregated job
categories, a comparison of the percentage of
minorities or women in an employer's work force
with the percentage in the area labor market or
general population is appropriate for jobs requiring
no special expertise or for training programs
designed to provide expertise. If a job requires

special training, a comparison should be made with the percentage of those in the labor force who possess the relevant qualifications. (*Paul E. Johnson v. Transportation Agency, Santa Clara County, California, et al.*, No. 107 S. Ct. 1444 [1987].)

Justice Antonin Scalia in a dissenting opinion pointed out that the *Johnson* decision effectively replaced the goal of a discrimination-free society with "the quite incompatible goal of proportionate representation by race and by sex in the workplace." There seems to be no consensus whether the elimination of prior discrimination justifies another kind of state-enforced discrimination. Discrimination in reverse is not a solution, because two wrongs do not make a right, but there are no doubts that we have made enormous progress in seeking equality. To realize the extent of this progress we may be reminded of the letter Abigail Adams wrote to her husband, John, at the Continental Congress: "[B]y the way, in the new Code of Laws . . . I desire you would remember the ladies and be more generous and favorable to them, than were your ancestors. . . . Remember, all men would be tyrants if they could." To which he replied, "Depend upon it, we men know better than to repeal our masculine systems." (*The Book of Abigail and John: Selected Letters of the Adams Family, 1762–1784*, Ed. by L. H. Butterfield, Marc Friedlaender, and Mary-Jo Kline, Harvard University Press, 1975, pp. 121, 123.) The repeal, however, has now taken place in some degree.

Tensions Between Freedom and Equality

Although in the history of our nation there are

pages of racism and discrimination, the voice of national conscience has constantly evoked the image of America as a moral society with a potential for redemption and a desire to remedy anything profoundly wrong. The founders of this nation, with compelling clarity, projected an image of America where not merely some but all people are created with equal rights and where their basic rights are neither conferred by nor derived from the state. This image has the magnetic power that attracts people from all parts of the world to our shores to rejoice in the deep-rooted tradition of the idea that every human being is the heir of the legacy of worthiness left to this world by the Old and New Testaments.

In spite of the sweeping changes in the outlook on equality in our nation, the hope for complete equality in freedom is dimmed by the tension that seems inherently to exist between freedom and equality as a paradoxical condition of democracy. Equality in freedom has a tendency to slip at the moment when we think that democratic institutions are mature enough to grasp it.

The reality of equality in freedom falls short of the dreams which inspired it, primarily because of the confusion about the meaning of freedom and equality in a free society. Glaring hypocrisies result from pushing the ideas of freedom and equality to their extremes. One extreme is the concept of absolute freedom. The other extreme is the egalitarian concept that all people are created equal in every respect, illustrated by the popular appeal of Louisiana Governor Huey Long's slogan of "every man a king." Total freedom is the law of the jungle, where only the fiercest, the strongest, and the most ruthless survive. Freedom is not absolute and is justified only if in pursuing our own interests we do not deprive others of theirs or impede their efforts to obtain it. Regarding equality, much restlessness can be traced to the misguided belief that equal opportunity means equality of success, uniformity, equally distributed rewards, and a guarantee of an absolute equality of results.

By the same token, equality of opportunity does not mean a license for the unrestrained, monopolistic accumulation of wealth. In the field of economics, the concentration of power in the hands of a few is an insidious menace to unfettered competition and an assault upon equal opportunities. Some scholars and jurists, including Justice Louis Brandeis, have spoken of monopolies as "the negation of industrial democracy." The aggregation of capital in the hands of a few individuals or corporations presents, in the words of Justice Harlan, a real danger of "slavery to be fostered on the American people." The accumulation of enormous fortunes is a radical departure from the idea of freedom in which economic and political equality can flourish. It is a half-understood truth, if not irresponsible demagoguery, to maintain that economic centralization leaves open the chance of free trade and competition. In reality, through monopolistic pressures, it eliminates equal competition and escapes the risks to its own privileges that would flow from equal opportunities for the man in the street.

Equality Versus Egalitarianism

No less dangerous than economic overcentralization is the failure to distinguish between equality before the law and the vicious perversion of equality that arises from the claim that all people have equal talents, equal mental and physical strength, and an equal desire to succeed. The wishful thinking that all individuals are born with equal abilities deepens the conflict between liberty and equal opportunities. Only totalitarian rulers offer a complete equality in mediocrity, which reduces all people down to the level of helplessness and impotence before the power of the government. Complete equality, by eliminating competition, eliminates also opportunities to all who can profitably use them.

The French Revolution of 1789 in its *Declaration of the Rights of Man and of Citizens* declared, "The law is an expression of the will of the community . . . and all being equal in its sight, are equally eligible to all honours, places, and employments, according to their different abilities, without any other distinction than that created by their virtue and talents." The slogan calling for open competition to public appointments was "La carrière ouverte aux talents" (Careers open to talents).

President Lincoln, referring to the signers of the Declaration of Independence, commented:

"The authors of that notable instrument . . . did not intend to declare all men equal in all respects. They did not mean to say that all men were equal in color, size, intellect, moral development, or social capacity. They defined with tolerable distinctness in what respect they consider all men created equal—'certain inalienable rights, among which are life, liberty, and the pursuit of happiness.' "

Happiness is not conferred upon mankind by the Creator, as life and liberty are. Man has the right to pursue happiness, and this right does not imply that all men and women are created equal in talent nor that they should be rewarded equally by society. People are not products of cloning, and equality should not be confused with uniformity. Under uniform standardization, outstanding achievements are frowned on and excellence is punished.

Equality in freedom means that (1) opportunities will be afforded to all persons in a free society where arbitrary or artificial barriers based on birth, economic status, race, religion, or sex do not exist; (2) in the open competition for scarce opportunities it is the responsibility of each person to apply himself or herself to the pursuit of such opportunities; and (3) the exceptional performance or industriousness, the extra efforts, and the special abilities that result in a high quality of goods or services should be rewarded.

Individual superiority, not uniform standardization; the use of people's abilities to the fullest limits of their capacity, not mediocrity; freedom to gain individual achievements by one's own efforts, not a subservience to egalitarianism—these will secure the progress and the prosperity that depend upon the continuous strengthening of excellence. A nation's

long-term interest demands the rejection both of
uniformity as the standard of performance and of
the "egalitarian doctrine of justice." Our society has
the responsibility to accept equal opportunity as an
unquestionable right and to provide equal opportunity to all, based on capability, diligence, and performance. This passion for justice and equality is
paralleled by the responsibility to push forward our
intellectual forces to the highest level and to disregard the erroneous egalitarian doctrine of justice
that calls for equality of results and rewards. By
reconciling these two responsibilities, equality and
freedom form an inseparable relationship.

The "New Egalitarians," who promulgate the doctrine of equality of results, expect the federal government to be "responsible not only for the total amount
of national income, but for its distribution. . . ."
(Christopher Jencks, *Inequality*, Basic Books, 1972,
p. 264.) Equality, they argue, "cannot be defined
solely in terms of opportunity, it must also be judged
by results, by whether current inequalities of income
and wealth, occupation, political power and the like
are being reduced." (Herbert J. Gans, *More Equality*,
Pantheon Books, 1973, p. xi.) In order to carry out
the radically equal distribution of "all social primary
goods," which also include "bases of social respect,"
such as social position, income, property, and rank,
the "accidents of natural endowment" should be nul-
lified. (John Rawls, *A Theory of Justice*, Belknap Press,
Harvard, 1971, p. 15.)

The equality of results recommended by the New
Egalitarians leans toward what Tocqueville called
"the new despotism." He had this kind of equality

in mind when he wrote that in order to succeed in centralizing the supreme power, the sole precondition required is to get people to believe that they love equality. According to Tocqueville, the single principle of the science of despotism is, "Every central power which follows its natural tendencies courts and encourages the principle of equality; for equality singularly facilitates, extends, and secures this influence of a central power." Egalitarian justice, by vesting in the government the responsibility for equal distribution of income and wealth, not only sacrifices economic expediency and the need for incentives but, what is more important, destroys our freedom, thus bringing into focus the central cause of the tension between liberty and equality.

Political Equality

People seek economic equality in the sense of enjoying a decent income, so as to provide the minimum needs of their families, such as decent shelter, decent educational opportunity, decent health care, and decent retirement benefits. They also seek political equality as well as civic and social equality. Political equality calls for an effective sharing of the political process that shapes the life of the community, of the state, and of the nation. It demands an opportunity for every citizen to participate in government on equal terms with everyone else. One of the landmark decisions in this field was the *Charles W. Baker v. Joe C. Carr* decision of March 26, 1962 (82 S. Ct. 691), which gave urban voters underrepresented in the state legislature a justiciable constitutional cause of action.

Until 1962 the courts had refused to intervene in controversies concerning the standards of fairness for a representative system. They had argued that it was beyond their competence to revise congressional representative districts in order to reflect the great changes that had taken place in the distribution of a state's population. The widely heralded case of *Colegrove v. Green* (66 S. Ct. 1198), which in the words of Justice Ramsey Clark had "served as Mother Hubbard to most of the subsequent cases" before *Baker v. Carr*, illustrates the now-abandoned position of the Supreme Court not to take action on issues of "a peculiarly political nature," such as legislative apportionment.

The following facts were essential to the *Colegrove v. Green* case. The Illinois legislature in 1901 established congressional election districts on the basis of the 1900 census. The state legislature was chosen on the basis of state election districts apportioned in a way similar to that of the 1901 congressional election districts. The federal census of 1910, of 1920, of 1930, and of 1940 each showed a great population shift among the districts established in 1901. But all attempts to have the state legislature reapportion congressional districts so as more nearly to equalize their population had been unsuccessful. Consequently, the congressional election districts had populations that ranged from 112,000 to 914,000. Three petitioners, citizens of Illinois, claimed that since they lived in the heavily populated districts, their vote was far less effective than that of people living in a much more sparsely populated district who also were allowed to choose one Congressman (some smaller districts were only one-ninth the population of some heavily populated districts). The petitioners contended that this reduction of the effectiveness of their vote resulted in legislative discrimination against them and thus amounted to a denial of the equal protection of the laws guaranteed by the Fourteenth Amendment.

The Supreme Court affirmed the dismissal of the complaint by the district court. Justice Felix Frankfurter, who announced the judgment, stated in his opinion that the Constitution precludes jurisdiction in this case since Article I, Section 4, has conferred upon Congress exclusive authority to secure fair representation by the states in the popular House and left to that House the determination of whether states have fulfilled their responsibility. (Article I, Section 4, provides that "the Times, Places and Manner of Holding Elections for . . . Representatives, shall be prescribed in each State by the Legislature thereof; but the Congress may at any time by Law make or alter such Regulations. . . .") Consequently, the subject of whether Congress faithfully discharges its duty, argued Justice Frankfurter, has been committed to the exclusive control of Congress, and the judiciary has been "excluded by the clear intention of the Constitution." (Justices Stanley F. Reed and Harold H. Burton concurred with Justice Frankfurter's opinion.)

In a dissenting opinion, Justice Hugo Black pointed out that the Equal Protection Clause of the Fourteenth Amendment forbids discrimination that gives certain citizens a fractional vote and others a full vote. He agreed that such discrimination was taking place in Illinois. This discrimination, argued Justice Black, violated Article I of the Constitution, which provides that Congressmen "shall be . . . chosen . . . by the People of the several States," and Section 2 of the Fourteenth Amendment, which provides that "Representatives shall be apportioned among the several States according to their respective numbers. . . ." In Justice Black's judgment, the courts, under the Constitution, have jurisdiction over geographical distribution of electoral strength among the state's political subdivisions. (Justice Black was joined in his dissent by Justices William O. Douglas and Frank Murphy; Justice John Rutledge, writing separately, expressed agreement with Justice Black's conclusion.)

The principle of equality before the law—which applies also to political equality—demanded the settlement of two controversial questions: First, should the Supreme Court intervene in matters of apportionment when the history of congressional apportionment "is its embroilment in politics, in the sense of party contests and party interest," and, second, is the right of every citizen to have an equally effective voice in electing his or her representatives— which is a right essential under a free government—a constitutional and federally protected right, and should the federal courts therefore provide a remedy to rectify any wrong done? The controversy aroused by these questions was settled by the U. S. Supreme Court in its decision of *Baker v. Carr* and in the one-person, one-vote decision of *Reynolds v. Sims* (377 U. S. 533 [1964].)

The facts in *Baker v. Carr* were similar to those in
Colegrove v. Green (although in the latter case the appellants did not present an equal protection argument). In 1901 the Tennessee General Assembly,
relying upon the federal census, passed an apportionment act. In the more than 60 years since that action,
all reapportionment proposals in both Houses and
the General Assembly had failed to pass in spite of
the fact that, since 1901, Tennessee had experienced
substantial growth and redistribution of population.
The relative standings of the counties in terms of
qualified voters also had changed substantially.

The complaint alleged that the 1901 statute had
denied the appellants (plaintiffs in the district court)
the equal protection of the laws accorded them by
the Fourteenth Amendment to the Constitution "by
virtue of the debasement of their votes." According
to Justice Clark the apportionment in Tennessee was
"a topsy-turvical of gigantic proportions . . . a crazy
quilt without rational basis." The district court dismissed the case on two grounds: (1) that the court
lacked jurisdiction over the subject matter and
(2) that the complaint failed to state a claim upon
which relief could be granted. The district court
proceeded to explain that from a review of numerous Supreme Court decisions there could be no
doubt that federal courts, "whether from lack of jurisdiction or from the inappropriateness of the subject
matter for judicial consideration, will not intervene in cases of this type to compel legislative
reapportionment."

The U. S. Supreme Court reversed the judgment
of the district court, and the case was remanded for

further proceedings consistent with the opinion delivered by Justice William Brennan. The Supreme Court held that a complaint containing allegations that a state statute effected an apportionment that deprived certain citizens of equal protection of the laws in violation of the Fourteenth Amendment presented an appropriate subject for judicial consideration.

Article III, Section 2, of the federal Constitution provides that "the judicial Power shall extend to all Cases, in Law and Equity, arising under this Constitution, the Laws of the United States, and Treaties made, or which shall be made, under their authority. . . ." The complaint alleged that the 1901 statute effected an apportionment that deprived the appellants of the equal protection of the law in violation of the Fourteenth Amendment, and, therefore, in the opinion of the Court there was a cause of action which "arises under" the federal Constitution. (Dismissal of the complaint upon the ground of lack of jurisdiction over the subject matter would be justified only if that claim were "so attenuated and unsubstantial as to be absolutely devoid of merit.")

The Court, by deciding that a citizen's right to vote is secured by the Constitution and that federal courts have jurisdiction over controversies concerning voting rights, did not imply that state legislatures must be so structured as to reflect with approximate equality the voice of every voter. There is no requirement that an apportionment plan must have mathematical exactness in its application. Only, as Justice Clark stated in a concurring opinion, where the total picture "reveals incommensurables of both magnitude and frequency can it be said that there is present an invidious discrimination."

The *Baker v. Carr* decision that apportionment cases present a justiciable controversy subject to adjudication by federal courts opened the door to challenges to existing apportionment plans under the Equal Protection Clause of the Fourteenth Amendment. The Supreme Court addressed the merits of six cases decided two years later, in 1964, announcing the "one-person, one-vote" requirement, which demanded that state legislative districts should be apportioned on the basis of population. The leading decision was issued in the case *B. A. Reynolds v. M. O. Sims*, involving legislative apportionment in Alabama. (377 U. S. 533 [1964].)

The plaintiffs in this case, residents and taxpayers of Jefferson County, noted that the last apportionment of the Alabama legislature was based on the 1900 federal census. They claimed that since population growth in the state from 1900 to 1960 had been uneven, numerous counties were victims of discrimination with respect to the allocation of legislative representation. Applying 1960 figures, only 25.9 percent of the state's total population resided in districts represented by a majority of the members of the Senate. Population variance ratios of up to about 41-to-1 existed in the Senate and up to about 16-to-1 in the House. Thus Jefferson County, with more than 600,000 people, was given only one senator, as were Lowndes County, with a 1960 population of only 15,417, and Wilcox County, with only 18,739. With respect to the allocation of seats in the Alabama House, Mobile County, with a population of 314,301,

was given three seats and Jefferson County, with
634,864 people, had seven, whereas Bullock County,
with a population of only 13,426, and Henry County,
with only 15,286, were allocated two seats each.

On July 12, 1962, the Alabama legislature adopted
two reapportionment plans to take effect for the 1966
elections. One, referred to as the "67-Senator Amendment," provided for a House of Representatives consisting of 106 members, apportioned by giving one
seat to each of Alabama's 67 counties and distribut-
ing the others according to population by the "equal
proportions" method. The Senate was to be composed of 67 members, one from each county.

The other reapportionment plan, referred to as the
Crawford-Webb Act, provided for a Senate consisting
of 35 members, representing 35 senatorial districts
established along county lines. In apportioning the
106 seats in the Alabama House of Representatives,
the act gave each county one seat and apportioned
the remaining 39 on a population basis.

On July 21, 1962, the district court considered both
the 67-Senator Amendment and the Crawford-Webb
Act and concluded that they were totally unacceptable since neither of them met the necessary constitutional requirements. The court found that each of
the legislative acts was discriminatory, arbitrary, and
irrational. In reference to the so-called federal analogy of senatorial apportionment based on a geographical basis, the court found it irrelevant because
of the dramatically opposing history of the requirements of the federal Constitution and the Alabama
Constitution.

On July 25, 1962, the court—directing its concern

to finding a remedy—ordered into effect for the November 1962 election a provisional and temporary reapportionment phase composed of the 67-Senator Amendment provisions relating to the House of Representatives and the Crawford-Webb Act provisions relating to the Senate. The court emphasized that its action would not suffice as a permanent reapportionment. The court also enjoined state officials from holding future elections under any of the apportionment plans that it had found invalid.

The plaintiffs and the defendants appealed the decision of the district court to the Supreme Court of the United States. On June 15, 1964, the Supreme Court held that the existing apportionment and the two proposed legislative plans for reapportionment of the seats in the two houses of the Alabama legislature were invalid under the Equal Protection Clause in that the apportionment was not based on population and was completely lacking in rationality. The Court affirmed the judgment of the district court and remanded the cases for further proceedings consistent with the views stated in the opinion.

The Court's opinion stressed the undeniable, constitutionally protected right of all qualified citizens to vote, in state as well as in federal elections. The right of suffrage is a fundamental matter in a free and democratic society. Legislators, stated the Court, "represent people, not trees or acres. . . . Legislators are elected by voters, not farms or economic interests." Considerations of area alone provide, therefore, "an insufficient justification for deviations from the equal-population principle." This principle is fundamental for a representative government.

Equal representation for equal numbers of people and the right to vote freely for candidates of one's choice are the essence of a democratic society. The district court did not err, stated the Supreme Court, in holding that neither of the two proposed plans to remedy the existing crazy-quilt apportionment in Alabama met the necessary constitutional require- ments. The Supreme Court agreed with the district court that no conceivable analogy could be drawn between the federal scheme of allocating two Senate seats in the federal Congress to each of the 50 states, regardless of population, and the apportionment of seats in the Alabama legislature under the proposed 67-Senator Amendment.

The system of representation in the two Houses of the federal Congress was one conceived out of compromise and concessions in order to avert a deadlock in the Constitutional Convention that had threatened to abort the birth of our nation. In estab- lishing federalism, the formerly independent states bound themselves under one national government. It was not their intention to establish a pattern for the apportionment of seats in state legislatures. Counties, cities, or other political subdivisions serve as subordinates to the state governmental instrumen- talities created by a state to assist in carrying out governmental functions. They were never considered as independently sovereign entities. Therefore, stated the Court, the 67-Senator Amendment for apportion- ing seats in the Alabama legislature could not be sustained by recourse to the so-called federal analogy and did not meet the requirements of the Equal

Protection Clause. The Supreme Court concluded, however, that the action taken by the district court, ordering into effect a reapportionment of both houses of the Alabama Legislature for purposes of the 1962 primary elections by using the best parts of the two proposed plans (which the Court found, as a whole, to be invalid), was "an appropriate and well considered exercise of judicial power."

The plan ordered by the district court was intended only as a temporary and provisional measure, not to be sustained as the basis for conducting the 1966 election of the Alabama legislature. Further evidence of an appropriate exercise of judicial power, stated the Supreme Court, is the intent of the district court to take some additional action should the reapportioned Alabama legislature "fail to enact a constitutionally valid, permanent apportionment scheme in the interim. . . ."

As Justice Clark, who concurred in the Supreme Court decision, pointed out, the "equal population" principle for state legislative apportionment discussed above is an "offshoot" of the one-person, one-vote principle that the Supreme Court stated in *Gray v. Sanders*: "The conception of political equality from the Declaration of Independence, to Lincoln's Gettysburg Address, to the Fifteenth, Seventeenth, and Nineteenth Amendments can mean only one thing—one person, one vote." (372 U. S. 368, 381 [1963].)

The *Wesberry v. Sanders* decision, built upon *Gray v. Sanders*, stated that congressional representation must be based on population "as nearly as is practicable." (376 U. S. 1, 8 [1964].) Without diluting the equal-population principle, more flexibility may be constitutionally permissible in legislative apportionment than in congressional districting because of the significantly larger number of seats in the state legislative bodies to be distributed within a state.

In numerous other decisions the Supreme Court ascertained that there are no cognizable principles that would justify a departure from the basic standard of equality among voters in the apportionment of seats in state legislatures. Diluting the weight of votes because of place of residence, economic status, or race impairs basic constitutional rights under the Fourteenth Amendment and strikes at the heart of representative government. The Equal Protection Clause demands substantially equal state legislative representation for all citizens in all places and of all races.

This right of voters to judicial protection under the Equal Protection Clause remade the political map of the United States and brought a political balance between urban and rural areas. (At the time of the one-person, one-vote decisions, rural areas held, nationwide, nearly twice as many legislative seats as they would have been entitled to by an apportionment based on the equal-population principle.)

It should be mentioned that before the case of *Baker v. Carr* reversed a uniform course of decision established by numerous earlier cases, the Supreme Court applied the Fifteenth Amendment to strike down a redrafting of municipal boundaries which effected a discriminatory impairment of voting rights. In the case of *Gomillion v. Lightfoot*, the plaintiff, Gomillion—a Negro who had been a resident of

Tuskogee, Alabama, until the municipal boundaries were so recast by the state legislature as to exclude practically all Negroes—claimed deprivation of the right to vote in municipal elections. (364 U. S. 339 [1960].)

The Supreme Court unanimously reversed the decision of the district court, which had been affirmed by the court of appeals for want of jurisdiction and a failure to state a claim upon which relief could be granted. In response to the argument (endorsed by *Colegrove v. Green*) that states enjoyed unrestricted control over municipal boundaries, the Court responded that Gomillion was lifted "out of the so-called 'political' arena and into the conventional sphere of constitutional litigation" because there was discriminatory treatment of a racial minority, which violated the Fifteenth Amendment. State power exercised within the domain of state interest may be insulated from federal judicial review, but, stated the Court, "such insulation is not carried over when state power is used as an instrument for circumventing a federally protected right." (*Gomillion v. Lightfoot, Ibid.*, p. 347.)

The right to vote is inherent in the republican form of government envisaged by Article IV, Section 4, of the Constitution. The Fifteenth and Nineteenth Amendments provide barriers to a state's freedom in prescribing qualifications of voters. Race, color, religion, and sex are impermissible standards that would permit a state to weight the vote of one county or one district more heavily than another. The Equal Protection Clause does not permit a state legislature to discriminate against the "underrepresented" counties or districts in favor of the "overrepresented" counties or districts in the collection and distribution of various taxes, tax revenues, and school and highway improvement funds. Legislators have no immunity from the Constitution; they are, stated the Court, "as responsive to the Constitution of the United States as are the citizens who elect [them]."

The fact that federal courts have jurisdiction over controversies concerning voting rights does not turn them into forums for political debate. The "right to have one's vote counted" is not a "political question" but one of civil rights, which include the right to vote, a right that lends itself to judicial standards and judicial remedies. The chief function of the courts, as John Rutledge (later Chief Justice) stated about 200 years ago in the course of the Constitutional Convention, is to secure the national rights. The right to vote, indispensable for the representative form of government, is one of these national rights and fundamental principles upon which our government is based.

Civil, Legal, and Social Equality

Among the types of equality that people seek and achieve by overthrowing the barriers of race and sex and in which our society seems greatly interested are civil, or legal, and social equalities. The right to serve on juries or the right to belong to associations of a person's own choosing are examples of such equalities. The courts and civil rights legislation press for constitutional prohibitions of discriminational practices and for the removal of conditions under which people cannot enjoy equal power in participation in group life.

As early as in 1880 the Supreme Court struck down a state statute that denied to Negroes on account of race participation as jurors in the administration of justice. Such a statute was held to contravene the main purpose of the Fourteenth Amendment. The very fact, wrote the Court,

> "that colored people are singled out and expressly denied by a statute all right to participate in the administration of the law, as jurors, because of their color, though they are citizens, and may be in other respects fully qualified, is practically a brand upon them, affixed by the law, an assertion of their inferiority, and a stimulant to that race prejudice which is an impediment to securing to individuals of the race that equal justice which the law aims to secure to all others." (*Strauder v. State of Virginia*, 100 U. S. 308 [1880].)

This set of principles was explicitly reaffirmed and repeatedly applied in many cases coming before the Court. These well-established principles include the prima facie proof of systematic discrimination when citizens because of race are excluded from jury service for an extended period of time. This "rule of exclusion" became an indisputable fact in a case, for instance, when no black had served on a jury for a period of 30 years. When such a situation occurred, stated the Court, "it became the duty of the State to try to justify such an exclusion as having been brought about for some reason other than racial discrimination." (*Patton v. State of Mississippi*, 332 U. S. 466 [1947]; see also the case of *Hernandez v. State of Texas*, 347 U. S. 480 [1954].)

Racial discrimination that results in the exclusion from jury service of otherwise qualified groups because of their race not only violates our Constitution but, as the Court stated, "is at war with our basic concepts of a democratic society and a representative government." (*Smith v. State of Texas*, 311 U. S. 128, 130 [1940].)

Also at war with our basic concepts of democracy are discriminatory practices conflicting with social equality—practices that deny any person full access to publicly available goods and services. Since social equality demands such access, the question arose whether this access should extend to private organizations' membership practices. Some have sought to find shelter for these practices, which quite often have been discriminatory, under the umbrella of the First Amendment.

It is beyond debate that freedom of association is an indispensable means of preserving other individual liberties assured by the First Amendment, which embraces freedom of speech, assembly, petition for redress of grievances, and the exercise of religion. Although the word "association" is not listed among the constitutionally protected rights, the Supreme Court has repeatedly acknowledged freedom of association as one of the rights derived by implication from the written First Amendment guarantees.

Finding an answer to the question of whether the commitment to social equality applies also to membership practices of private organizations required the courts to address the conflict between a state's effort to eliminate discrimination on the basis of gender, race, nationality, origin, or religion against its citizens seeking membership in private organizations and the constitutional freedom of association asserted by members of these private organizations.

In one line of decisions, the Supreme Court has concluded that certain intimate human relationships must be secured against intrusion by the state because of the role of such relationships in safeguarding the individual freedoms that are essential to our form of government. Interference by the state with individuals' selection of whom they wish to join in a common endeavor for the advancement of beliefs and ideas or with whom they have strong personal bonds may violate the guaranteed freedom of association.

In another set of decisions, the Court has recognized a right to associate with others in pursuit of a wide variety of political, social, economic, educational, religious, and cultural needs. This right reflects the commitment to eliminating discrimination because of race, color, creed, religion, national origin, or sex and to assuring its citizens equal access and enjoyment of publicly available goods, services, and facilities.

The right to social equality is not absolute, since it comes in contact with boundaries of the right to associate with others. Within the broad range of human relationships, there are certain zones of privacy, such as marriage, procreation, contraception, cohabitation with relatives, or child rearing and education, that are protected from government interference. On the other hand, there are innumerable commercial associations that enjoy a minimal constitutional protection since their activities are not predominantly of the type protected by the First Amendment. For instance, according to the U. S. Supreme Court, chapters of the United States Jaycees and of Rotary International lack the distinctive characteristics that may afford constitutional protection to the decision of their members to exclude women.

The United States Jaycees is a nonprofit national membership corporation whose objective is to pursue such educational and charitable purposes as will promote and foster the growth and development of young men's civic organizations. Regular membership is limited to young men between ages 18 and 35, whereas women may purchase only associate membership. An associate member may not vote, hold local or national office, or receive achievement awards. In 1974, the Minneapolis and St. Paul, Minnesota, local chapters had, in defiance of the bylaws, admitted women as regular members and, as a result, had had a number of sanctions imposed by the national organization of the Jaycees. When those two local chapters were informed that revocation of their charters was to be considered, members of both chapters filed discrimination charges with the Minnesota Department of Human Rights, challenging the Jaycees' policy of forbidding women the same membership status as men.

The Minnesota Human Rights Act forbids discrimination on the basis of sex in "places of public accommodation." The United States District Court upheld the application of the act to the Jaycees. The Court of Appeals for the Eighth Circuit reversed the decision, holding that the application of the act to the Jaycees would produce a "direct and substantial" interference with the Jaycees' freedom of association guaranteed by the First Amendment and that the act was vague as construed and applied and hence unconstitutional under the Due Process Clause of the Fourteenth Amendment.

The U. S. Supreme Court reversed the judgment of the court of appeals by taking the position that the individual's rights provided by the First Amendment could not be protected from interference by the state "unless a correlative freedom to engage in group effort toward those ends were not also guaranteed." Therefore, the Court stated, because of the compelling interest in eradicating discrimination against women, the application of the Minnesota act to the Jaycees forcing it to accept women as regular members does not abridge either the male members' freedom of intimate association or their freedom of expressive association. The Court also did not find the Minnesota Human Rights Act unconstitutionally vague, because it articulates its aims with a reasonable degree of clarity. (*Kathryn R. Roberts v. United States Jaycees*, 468 U. S. 609 [1984].)

The Supreme Court took a similar position in the case of *Board of Directors of Rotary International v. Rotary Club of Duarte.* (107 S. Ct. 1940 [1987].) Rotary International is a nonprofit corporation composed of local Rotary Clubs. It is an "organization of business and professional men united worldwide who provide humanitarian service, encourage high ethical standards in all vocations, and help build goodwill and peace in the world." Membership in Rotary Clubs is open only to men. Although women are permitted to attend meetings, give speeches, receive awards, and form auxiliary organizations, the Rotary constitution excludes women from membership.

In 1977 the Rotary Club of Duarte, California, admitted three women to active membership, and the board of directors of Rotary International revoked its charter and terminated its membership in Rotary International. The Duarte Club and two of its women members filed a complaint in the California Superior Court for the County of Los Angeles. The court found that Rotary Clubs do not provide their members with goods, services, or facilities and that business benefits are only incidental to the principal purposes of the association. Consequently, the court entered judgment for Rotary International.

The California Court of Appeals reversed this judgment. It held that the California Superior Court had erred in finding that the business advantages afforded by membership in a local Rotary Club are merely incidental. The court of appeals also rejected the trial court's finding that the Duarte Club does not provide goods, services, or facilities to its members. Rotary Clubs, rather than carrying on their activities in an atmosphere of privacy, seek to keep their "windows and doors open to the world." By opening membership to leading business and professional women, stated the Supreme Court when it reviewed the case, Rotary Clubs "are likely to obtain a more representative cross-section of community leaders with a broadened capacity for service." As in the *Roberts* case, the U. S. Supreme Court stressed that the state's compelling interest in assuring equal access to women extends to the acquisition of leadership skills and business contacts as well as tangible goods and services. The judgment of the Court of Appeals of California was affirmed.

In the light of the two U. S. Supreme Court decisions described above, the definition of goods, services, and public accommodations reaches various forms of public and quasi-commercial conduct. This expansive definition, stated the Court in the *Roberts* case, "reflects a recognition of the changing nature of the American economy and of the importance, both to the individual and to society, of removing both barriers to economic advancement and political and social integration that have historically plagued certain disadvantaged groups, including women."

Equality Among Nations

The recognition of the importance of "removing the barriers" to the advancement of equality goes beyond national boundaries. Human dignity—the essential working principle of equality—when applied to international relations means faith in the dignity of each nation, poor or opulent, militarily powerful or weak. It means progress in the direction of a free family of nations safeguarded by the rule of law and the principle of equality before the law.

Equality among nations was advocated by the French mathematician and philosopher Marie Jean Antoine Nicolas Caritat, Marquis de Condorcet, who took part in the French Revolution. He traced human development through nine epochs to the outbreak of the revolution and predicted the abolition of inequalities in the tenth epoch, which would follow the revolution. He argued that the rights of women should be equal with the rights of men and that freedom demanded the equality of rights among nations. (For opposing the cruelty of the Jacobins, Condorcet was put in prison, where he died.)

After World War I, the aim of peace through the equality of all nations was outlined by President Woodrow Wilson as follows: "No special or separate interest of any single nation or any group of nations can be made the basis of any part of the settlement which is not consistent with the common interest of all." (The "Five Particulars" of September 27, 1918.) "Every territorial settlement . . . must be made in the interest of and for the benefit of the populations concerned, and not as a part of any mere adjustment or compromise of claims among rival States." (The "Four Principles" of February 11, 1918.) After World War II, the peoples of Bulgaria, Czechoslovakia, Hungary, Poland, Rumania, and other "captive" nations could wonder whether their "equality" and destinies were not sacrificed on the altar of "compromise of claims among rival states" with disregard to the "benefit of the populations concerned."

Following World War II, human rights demanding economic and political equality were recognized by the Universal Declaration of Human Rights, approved by the United Nations General Assembly in 1948. The first group of human rights listed includes the right to the economic necessities of life and to fulfillment of such vital needs as food, shelter, health care, and education. The second group includes the opportunity to participate in one's government and the right to enjoy the civil and political liberties, such as freedom of thought, of assembly, of the press, of speech, of religion, and of moving freely both within and outside one's own country. These demands remained only words, proclaimed with no intention of enforcement.

The Charter of the United Nations provides that the General Assembly will assist "in the realization of human rights and fundamental freedoms for all without distinction as to race, sex, language, or religion. . . ." (Article 13.) The demands enshrined in the universal declaration enunciated by the General Assembly include the right to social security; to periodic holidays with pay; to security in the event of unemployment, sickness, disability, widowhood, old age, or lack of livelihood in circumstances beyond a person's control; and to an education that shall be free in the "elementary and fundamental stages" and other rights which in numerous countries have never become a fact and have remained an unobtainable ideal, with no expectation of any assistance from the General Assembly.

Strides in the Direction of Equality

To make equality work it is imperative to understand what equality is. The Declaration of Independence and the Constitution place great emphasis on liberty but take equality among individuals for granted, simply declaring that "all men are created equal." These historical documents do not refer to an equal distribution of income or to the removal of disparities of wealth. Equality of opportunity or equality before the law means the right to open competition and to a similarity of treatment under the rule of law, with all being equal in its sight.

Even such great historical documents—which are triumphs for the highest aspirations of mankind—remain mere words unless there is an understanding of their meaning and a willingness to act to implement them. In this country we have made great strides in the direction of equality, to mention only the progressive income tax; the public school system; the drive for equal voting privileges regardless of gender, race, or color; and such measures as Social Security, Medicare, the guaranteed minimum wage, old-age pensions, and recent civil rights legislation. There will always be a gap between what we want and what we can accomplish. There will always be a time for grander goals that seem to elude our grasp. The goals we have been seeking for so long, however, will never be achieved by confusing equality with an egalitarianism that decries excellence in achievement and that detracts from our national purpose. When its focus shifts from equality of opportunity to equality in the distribution of goods and services, the spirit of equality is destroyed.

Referring to the spirit of liberty, President Lincoln once said, "Our defense is in the spirit which prized liberty as the heritage of all men, in all lands, everywhere. Destroy this spirit and you have the seeds of despotism at your own front." Paraphrasing this warning we can say, "Destroy the spirit of equality by trying to assure for all equal income, equal wealth, equal position, equal power for mental development, and equal influence and you can expect to have 'the seeds of despotism at your own front.' "